Miscellaneous Poems by William Lisle Bowles

William Lisle Bowles was born on 24th September 1762 at King's Sutton in Northamptonshire.

His great-grandfather, grandfather and his father, William Thomas Bowles, had all been parish priests and inevitably Bowles would join their line.

In 1789 Bowles published, a small quarto volume, Fourteen Sonnets, which was received with extraordinary praise, not only by the general public, but by such revered poets as Samuel Taylor Coleridge and Wordsworth.

After receiving his degree at Oxford, Bowles now began his career in service to the Church of England.

His years of service perhaps diminished both his stature as a poet and certainly the way he was viewed. For much of his career Bowles was seen as rather soft when set against his contemporaries but in the end his ability as a poet was enshrined, after a long and ferocious attack against him, by the principles he so eloquently wrote about and adhered too.

In personality and nature Bowles was said to be an amiable, absent-minded, but rather eccentric man. His poems speak warmly of a refinement of feeling, tenderness, and pensive thought, but are lacking in power and passion. But that should not diminish their value or appreciation to us.

Bowles maintained that images drawn from nature are poetically finer than those drawn from art; and that in the highest kinds of poetry the themes or passions handled should be of the general or elemental kind, and not the transient manners of any society.

As well as his poetry Bowles was also responsible for writing a Life of Bishop Ken (in two volumes, 1830–1831), Coombe Ellen and St. Michael's Mount (1798), The Battle of the Nile (1799), and The Sorrows of Switzerland (1801).

William Lisle Bowles died on April 7th, 1850 at the age of 87.

Index of Contents
Elegy written at the Hotwells, Bristol
Monody on Henry Headley
Howard's Account of Lazarettos
The Grave of Howard
Shakspeare
Abbe Thule's Lament for his Son Prince Le Boo
Southampton Water
The Philanthropic Society
The Dying Slave
Song of the American Indian
Monody, written at Matlock
The Right Honourable Edmund Burke

On Leaving a Place of Residence
Elegiac Stanzas written during Sickness at Bath
On leaving Winchester School
Hope: an Allegorical Sketch
The Battle of the Nile
A Garden-Seat at Home
In Horto Rev. J. Still
Greenwich Hospital
A Rustic Seat near the Sea
Wardour Castle
Pole-vellum, Cornwall
On a Beautiful Spring
On a Cenotaph to the Memory of Lieut-Col. Isaac
Translation of a Latin Poem, by Rev. Newton Ogle
St Michael's Mount
On an Unfortunate and Beautiful Woman
Hymn to Woden
Coombe-Ellen
Summer Evening at Home
Winter Evening at Home
The Spirit of Navigation
Water-party on Beaulieu River, in the New Forest
Monody on the Death of Dr Warton
Epitaph on H. Walmsley, Esq., in Alverstokea Church, Hants
Age
On a Landscape by Rubens
The Harp, and Despair, of Cowper
Stanzas for Music
Music
Absence
Fairy Sketch
Inscription
Pictures from Theocritus
Sketches in the Exhibition, 1805
Sketches in the Exhibition, 1807
Southampton Castle
The Winds
On William Sommers of Bremhill
The Visionary Boy
Cadland, Southampton River
The Last Song of Camoens
The Sylph of Summer
The Harp of Hoel
Avenue in Savernake Forest
Dirge of Nelson
Death of Captain Cooke, of "The Bellerophon"
Battle of Corruna

Sketch from Bowden Hill after Sickness
Sun-Dial in the Churchyard of Bremhill
William Lisle Bowles – A Short Biography

ELEGY WRITTEN AT THE HOTWELLS, BRISTOL, INSCRIBED TO THE REV. W. HOWLEY

The morning wakes in shadowy mantle gray,
The darksome woods their glimmering skirts unfold,
Prone from the cliff the falcon wheels her way,
And long and loud the bell's slow chime is tolled.

The reddening light gains fast upon the skies,
And far away the glistening vapours sail,
Down the rough steep the accustomed hedger hies,
And the stream winds in brightness through the vale.

Mark how those riven rocks on either shore
Uplift their bleak and furrowed fronts on high;
How proudly desolate their foreheads hoar,
That meet the earliest sunbeams of the sky!

Bound for yon dusky mart, with pennants gay,
The tall bark, on the winding water's line,
Between the riven cliffs slow plies her way,
And peering on the sight the white sails shine.

Alas! for those by drooping sickness worn,
Who now come forth to meet the cheering ray;
And feel the fragrance of the tepid morn
Round their torn breasts and throbbing temples play!

Perhaps they muse with a desponding sigh
On the cold vault that shall their bones inurn;
Whilst every breeze seems, as it whispers by,
To breathe of comfort never to return.

Yet oft, as sadly thronging dreams arise,
Awhile forgetful of their pain they gaze,
A transient lustre lights their faded eyes,
And o'er their cheek the tender hectic plays.

The purple morn that paints with sidelong gleam
The cliff's tall crest, the waving woods that ring
With songs of birds rejoicing in the beam,
Touch soft the wakeful nerve's according string.

Then at sad Meditation's silent hour
A thousand wishes steal upon the heart;
And, whilst they meekly bend to Heaven's high power,
Ah! think 'tis hard, 'tis surely hard to part:

To part from every hope that brought delight,
From those that loved them, those they loved so much!
Then Fancy swells the picture on the sight,
And softens every scene at every touch.

Sweet as the mellowed woods beneath the moon,
Remembrance lends her soft-uniting shades;
"Some natural tears she drops, but wipes them soon:"—
The world retires, and its dim prospect fades!

Airs of delight, that soothe the aching sense;
Waters of health, that through yon caverns glide;
Oh! kindly yet your healing powers dispense,
And bring back feeble life's exhausted tide!

Perhaps to these gray rocks and mazy springs
Some heart may come, warmed with the purest fire;
For whom bright Fancy plumes her radiant wings,
And warbling Muses wake the lonely lyre.

Some orphan Maid, deceived in early youth,
Pale o'er yon spring may hang in mute distress;
Who dream of faith, of happiness, and truth,
Of love—that Virtue would protect and bless.

Some musing Youth in silence there may bend,
Untimely stricken by sharp Sorrow's dart;
For friendship formed, yet left without a friend,
And bearing still the arrow at his heart.

Such was lamented RUSSELL'S early doom,
The gay companion of our stripling prime;
Ev'n so he sank unwept into the tomb,
And o'er his head closed the dark gulph of time.

Hither he came, a wan and weary guest,
A softening balm for many a wound to crave;
And wooed the sunshine to his aching breast,
Which now seems smiling on his verdant grave!

He heard the whispering winds that now I hear,
As, boding much, along these hills he passed;
Yet ah! how mournful did they meet his ear

On that sad morn he heard them for the last!

So sinks the scene, like a departed dream,
Since late we sojourned blythe in Wykeham's bowers,
Or heard the merry bells by Isis' stream,
And thought our way was strewed with fairy flowers!

Of those with whom we played upon the lawn
Of early life, in the fresh morning played;
Alas! how many, since that vernal dawn,
Like thee, poor RUSSELL, 'neath the turf are laid!

Joyous a while they wandered hand in hand,
By friendship led along the springtide plain;
How oft did Fancy wake her transports bland,
And on the lids the glistening tear detain!

I yet survive, now musing other song,
Than that which early pleased my vacant years;
Thinking how days and hours have passed along,
Marked by much pleasure some, and some by tears!

Thankful, that to these verdant scenes I owe
That he whom late I saw all drooping pale,
Raised from the couch of sickness and of woe,
Now lives with me these mantling views to hail.

Thankful, that still the landscape beaming bright,
Of pendant mountain, or of woodland gray,
Can wake the wonted sense of pure delight,
And charm a while my solitary way.

Enough:—through the high heaven the proud sun rides,
My wandering steps their silent path pursue
Back to the crowded world where fortune guides:
Clifton, to thy white rocks and woods adieu!

MONODY ON HENRY HEADLEY

To every gentle Muse in vain allied,
In youth's full early morning HEADLEY died!
Too long had sickness left her pining trace,
With slow, still touch, on each decaying grace:
Untimely sorrow marked his thoughtful mien!
Despair upon his languid smile was seen!
Yet Resignation, musing on the grave,

(When now no hope could cheer, no pity save),
And Virtue, that scarce felt its fate severe,
And pale Affection, dropping soft a tear
For friends beloved, from whom she soon must part,
Breathed a sad solace on his aching heart.
Nor ceased he yet to stray, where, winding wild,
The Muse's path his drooping steps beguiled,
Intent to rescue some neglected rhyme,
Lone-blooming, from the mournful waste of time;
And cull each scattered sweet, that seemed to smile
Like flowers upon some long-forsaken pile.
Far from the murmuring crowd, unseen, he sought
Each charm congenial to his saddened thought.
When the gray morn illumed the mountain's side,
To hear the sweet birds' earliest song he hied;
When meekest eve to the fold's distant bell
Listened, and bade the woods and vales farewell,
Musing in tearful mood, he oft was seen
The last that lingered on the fading green.
The waving wood high o'er the cliff reclined,
The murmuring waterfall, the winter's wind,
His temper's trembling texture seemed to suit;
As airs of sadness the responsive lute.
Yet deem not hence the social spirit dead,
Though from the world's hard gaze his feelings fled:
Firm was his friendship, and his faith sincere,
And warm as Pity's his unheeded tear,
That wept the ruthless deed, the poor man's fate,
By fortune's storms left cold and desolate.
Farewell! yet be this humble tribute paid
To all his virtues, from that social shade
Where once we sojourned. I, alas! remain
To mourn the hours of youth, yet mourn in vain,
That fled neglected. Wisely thou hast trod
The better path; and that High Meed, which GOD
Ordained for Virtue towering from the dust,
Shall bless thy labours, spirit pure and just!

ON MR HOWARD'S ACCOUNT OF LAZARETTOS

Mortal! who, armed with holy fortitude,
The path of good right onward hast pursued;
May HE, to whose eternal throne on high
The sufferers of the earth with anguish cry,
Be thy protector!   On that dreary road
That leads thee patient to the last abode

Of wretchedness, in peril and in pain,
May HE thy steps direct, thy heart sustain!
'Mid scenes, where pestilence in darkness flies;
In caverns, where deserted misery lies;
So safe beneath His shadow thou may'st go,
To cheer the dismal wastes of human woe.
O CHARITY! our helpless nature's pride,
Thou friend to him who knows no friend beside,
Is there in morning's breath, or the sweet gale
That steals o'er the tired pilgrim of the vale,
Cheering with fragrance fresh his weary frame,
Aught like the incense of thy sacred flame?
Is aught in all the beauties that adorn
The azure heaven, or purple lights of morn;
Is aught so fair in evening's lingering gleam,
As from thine eye the meek and pensive beam
That falls like saddest moonlight on the hill
And distant grove, when the wide world is still!
Thine are the ample views, that unconfined
Stretch to the utmost walks of human kind:
Thine is the spirit that with widest plan
Brother to brother binds, and man to man.
But who for thee, O Charity! will bear
Hardship, and cope with peril and with care!
Who, for thy sake, will social sweets forego
For scenes of sickness, and the sights of woe!
Who, for thy sake, will seek the prison's gloom,
Where ghastly Guilt implores her lingering doom;
Where Penitence unpitied sits, and pale,
That never told to human ears her tale;
Where Agony, half-famished, cries in vain;
Where dark Despondence murmurs o'er her chain;
Where gaunt Disease is wasted to the bone,
And hollow-eyed Despair forgets to groan!
Approving Mercy marks the vast design,
And proudly cries—HOWARD, the task be thine!
Already 'mid the darksome vaults profound,
The inner prison deep beneath the ground,
Consoling hath thy tender look appeared:
In horror's realm the voice of peace is heard!
Be the sad scene disclosed; fearless unfold
The grating door—the inmost cell behold!
Thought shrinks from the dread sight; the paly lamp
Burns faint amid the infectious vapours damp;
Beneath its light full many a livid mien,
And haggard eye-ball, through the dusk are seen.
In thought I see thee, at each hollow sound,
With humid lids oft anxious gaze around.

But oh! for him who, to yon vault confined,
Has bid a long farewell to human kind;
His wasted form, his cold and bloodless cheek,
A tale of sadder sorrow seem to speak:
Of friends, perhaps now mingled with the dead;
Of hope, that, like a faithless flatterer, fled
In the utmost hour of need; or of a son
Cast to the bleak world's mercy; or of one
Whose heart was broken, when the stern behest
Tore him from pale affection's bleeding breast.
Despairing, from his cold and flinty bed,
With fearful muttering he has raised his head:
What pitying spirit, what unwonted guest,
Strays to this last retreat, these shades unblest?
From life and light shut out, beneath this cell
Long have I bid the cheering sun farewell.
I heard for ever closed the jealous door,
I marked my bed on the forsaken floor,
I had no hope on earth, no human friend:
Let me unpitied to the dust descend!
Cold is his frozen heart—his eye is reared
To Heaven no more—and on his sable beard
The tear has ceased to fall. Thou canst not bring
Back to his mournful heart the morn of spring;—
Thou canst not bid the rose of health renew
Upon his wasted cheek its crimson hue;
But at thy look, (ere yet to hate resigned,
He murmurs his last curses on mankind),
At thy kind look one tender thought shall rise,
And his full soul shall thank thee ere he dies!
Oh ye, who list to Pleasure's vacant song,
As in her silken train ye troop along;
Who, like rank cowards, from affliction fly,
Or, whilst the precious hours of life pass by,
Lie slumbering in the sun! Awake, arise,
To these instructive pictures turn your eyes;
The awful view with other feelings scan,
And learn from HOWARD what man owes to man!
These, Virtue! are thy triumphs, that adorn
Fitliest our nature, and bespeak us born
For loftier action; not to gaze and run
From clime to clime; nor flutter in the sun,
Dragging a droning flight from flower to flower,
Like summer insects in a gaudy hour;
Nor yet o'er love-sick tales with fancy range,
And cry—'Tis pitiful, 'tis wondrous strange!
But on life's varied views to look around,
And raise expiring sorrow from the ground:—

And he who thus has borne his part assigned
In the sad fellowship of human kind,
Or for a moment soothed the bitter pain
Of a poor brother, has not lived in vain!
But 'tis not that Compassion should bestow
An unavailing tear on want or woe:
Lo! fairer Order rises from thy plan,
Befriending virtue, and adorning man.
That Comfort cheers the dark abode of pain,
Where wan Disease prayed for relief in vain;
That Mercy soothes the hard behest of law;
That Misery smiles upon her bed of straw;
That the dark felon's clan no more, combined,
Murmur in murderous leagues against mankind;
That to each cell, a mild yet mournful guest,
Contrition comes, and calms the laboring breast,
Whilst long-forgotten tears of virtue flow;
Thou, generous friend of all—to thee we owe!
To thee, that Pity sees her views expand
To many a cheerless haunt, and distant land!
Whilst warm Philanthropy extends her ray,
Wide as the world, and general as the day!
HOWARD! I view those deeds, and think how vain
The triumphs of weak man, the feeble strain
That Flattery brings to Conquest's crimson car,
Amid the bannered host, and the proud tents of war!
From realm to realm the hideous War-fiend hies
Wide o'er the wasted earth; before him flies
Affright, on pinions fleeter than the wind;
Whilst Death and Desolation fast behind
The havoc of his echoing march pursue:
Meantime his steps are bathed in the warm dew
Of bloodshed, and of tears;—but his dread name
Shall perish—the loud clarion of his fame
One day shall cease, and, wrapt in hideous gloom,
Forgetfulness bestride his shapeless tomb!
But bear thou fearless on;—the God of all,
To whom the afflicted kneel, the friendless call,
From His high throne of mercy shall approve
The holy deeds of Mercy and of Love:
For when the vanities of life's brief day
Oblivion's hurrying wing shall sweep away,
Each act by Charity and Mercy done,
High o'er the wrecks of time, shall live alone,
Immortal as the heavens, and beauteous bloom
To other worlds, and realms beyond the tomb.

THE GRAVE OF HOWARD

Spirit of Death! whose outstretched pennons dread
Wave o'er the world beneath their shadow spread;
Who darkly speedest on thy destined way,
Midst shrieks and cries, and sounds of dire dismay;
Spirit! behold thy victory! Assume
A form more terrible, an ampler plume;
For he, who wandered o'er the world alone,
Listening to Misery's universal moan;
He who, sustained by Virtue's arm sublime,
Tended the sick and poor from clime to clime,
Low in the dust is laid, thy noblest spoil!
And Mercy ceases from her awful toil!
'Twas where the pestilence at thy command
Arose to desolate the sickening land,
When many a mingled cry and dying prayer
Resounded to the listening midnight air,
When deep dismay heard not the frequent knell,
And the wan carcase festered as it fell:
'Twas there, with holy Virtue's awful mien,
Amid the sad sights of that fearful scene,
Calm he was found: the dews of death he dried;
He spoke of comfort to the poor that cried;
He watched the fading eye, the flagging breath,
Ere yet the languid sense was lost in death;
And with that look protecting angels wear,
Hung o'er the dismal couch of pale Despair!
Friend of mankind! thy righteous task is o'er;
The heart that throbbed with pity beats no more.
Around the limits of this rolling sphere,
Where'er the just and good thy tale shall hear,
A tear shall fall: alone, amidst the gloom
Of the still dungeon, his long sorrow's tomb,
The captive, mourning, o'er his chain shall bend,
To think the cold earth holds his only friend!
He who with labour draws his wasting breath
On the forsaken silent bed of death,
Remembering thy last look and anxious eye,
Shall gaze around, unvisited, and die.
Friend of mankind, farewell! These tears we shed—
So nature dictates—o'er thy earthly bed;
Yet we forget not, it was His high will,
Who saw thee Virtue's arduous task fulfil,
Thy spirit from its toil at last should rest:—
So wills thy GOD, and what He wills is best!
Thou hast encountered dark Disease's train,

Thou hast conversed with Poverty and Pain,
Thou hast beheld the dreariest forms of woe,
That through this mournful vale unfriended go;
And, pale with sympathy, hast paused to hear
The saddest plaints e'er told to human ear.
Go then, the task fulfilled, the trial o'er,
Where sickness, want, and pain are known no more!
How awful did thy lonely track appear,
Enlightening Misery's benighted sphere!
As when an angel all-serene goes forth
To still the raging tempest of the north,
The embattled clouds that hid the struggling day,
Slow from his face retire in dark array;
On the black waves, like promontories hung,
A light, as of the orient morn, is flung,
Till blue and level heaves the silent brine,
And the new-lighted rocks at distance shine;
Ev'n so didst thou go forth with cheering eye—
Before thy glance the shades of misery fly;
So didst thou hush the tempest, stilling wide
Of human woe the loud-lamenting tide.
Nor shall the spirit of those deeds expire,
As fades the feeble spark of vital fire,
But beam abroad, and cheer with lustre mild
Humanity's remotest prospects wild,
Till this frail orb shall from its sphere be hurled,
Till final ruin hush the murmuring world,
And all its sorrows, at the awful blast
Of the archangel's trump, be but as shadows past!
Relentless Time, that steals with silent tread,
Shall tear away the trophies of the dead.
Fame, on the pyramid's aspiring top,
With sighs shall her recording trumpet drop;
The feeble characters of Glory's hand
Shall perish, like the tracks upon the sand;
But not with these expire the sacred flame
Of Virtue, or the good man's honoured name.
HOWARD! it matters not, that far away
From Albion's peaceful shore thy bones decay:
Him it might please, by whose sustaining hand
Thy steps were led through many a distant land.
Thy long and last abode should there be found,
Where many a savage nation prowls around:
That Virtue from the hallowed spot might rise,
And, pointing to the finished sacrifice,
Teach to the roving Tartar's savage clan
Lessons of love, and higher aims of man.
The hoary chieftain, who thy tale shall hear,

Pale on thy grave shall drop his faltering spear;
The cold, unpitying Cossack thirst no more
To bathe his burning falchion deep in gore;
Relentless to the cry of carnage speed,
Or urge o'er gasping heaps his panting steed!
Nor vain the thought that fairer hence may rise
New views of life, and wider charities.
Far from the bleak Riphean mountains hoar,
From the cold Don, and Wolga's wandering shore,
From many a shady forest's lengthening tract,
From many a dark-descending cataract,
Succeeding tribes shall come, and o'er the place,
Where sleeps the general friend of human race,
Instruct their children what a debt they owe;
Speak of the man who trode the paths of woe;
Then bid them to their native woods depart,
With new-born virtue stirring in their heart.
When o'er the sounding Euxine's stormy tides
In hostile pomp the Turk's proud navy rides,
Bent on the frontiers of the Imperial Czar,
To pour the tempest of vindictive war;
If onward to those shores they haply steer,
Where, HOWARD, thy cold dust reposes near,
Whilst o'er the wave the silken pennants stream,
And seen far off the golden crescents gleam,
Amid the pomp of war, the swelling breast
Shall feel a still unwonted awe impressed,
And the relenting Pagan turn aside
To think—on yonder shore the Christian died!
But thou, O Briton! doomed perhaps to roam
An exile many a year and far from home,
If ever fortune thy lone footsteps leads
To the wild Nieper's banks, and whispering reeds,
O'er HOWARD's grave thou shalt impassioned bend,
As if to hold sad converse with a friend.
Whate'er thy fate upon this various scene,
Where'er thy weary pilgrimage hath been,
There shalt thou pause; and shutting from thy heart
Some vain regrets that oft unbidden start,
Think upon him to every lot resigned,
Who wept, who toiled, and perished for mankind.
For me, who musing, HOWARD, on thy fate,
These pensive strains at evening meditate,
I thank thee for the lessons thou hast taught
To mend my heart, or animate my thought.
I thank thee, HOWARD, for that awful view
Of life which thou hast drawn, most sad, most true.
Thou art no more! and the frail fading bloom

Of this poor offering dies upon thy tomb.
Beyond the transient sound of earthly praise
Thy virtues live, perhaps, in seraph's lays!
I, borne in thought, to the wild Nieper's wave,
Sigh to the reeds that whisper o'er thy grave.

SHAKSPEARE

O sovereign Master! who with lonely state
Dost rule as in some isle's enchanted land,
On whom soft airs and shadowy spirits wait,
Whilst scenes of "faerie" bloom at thy command,
On thy wild shores forgetful could I lie,
And list, till earth dissolved to thy sweet minstrelsy!

Called by thy magic from the hoary deep,
Aërial forms should in bright troops ascend,
And then a wondrous masque before me sweep;
Whilst sounds, that the earth owned not, seem to blend
Their stealing melodies, that when the strain
Ceased, I should weep, and would so dream again!

The song hath ceased. Ah! who, pale shade, art thou,
Sad raving to the rude tempestuous night!
Sure thou hast had much wrong, so stern thy brow,
So piteous thou dost tear thy tresses white;
So wildly thou dost cry, Blow, bitter wind!
Ye elements, I call not you unkind!

Beneath the shade of nodding branches gray,
'Mid rude romantic woods, and glens forlorn,
The merry hunters wear the hours away;
Rings the deep forest to the joyous horn!
Joyous to all, but him, who with sad look
Hangs idly musing by the brawling brook.

But mark the merry elves of fairy land!
To the high moon's gleamy glance,
They with shadowy morrice dance;
Soft music dies along the desert sand;
Soon at peep of cold-eyed day,
Soon the numerous lights decay;
Merrily, now merrily,
After the dewy moon they fly.

The charm is wrought: I see an aged form,

In white robes, on the winding sea-shore stand;
O'er the careering surge he waves his wand:
Hark! on the bleak rock bursts the swelling storm:
Now from bright opening clouds I hear a lay,
Come to these yellow sands, fair stranger, come away!

Saw ye pass by the weird sisters pale!
Marked ye the lowering castle on the heath!
Hark, hark, is the deed done—the deed of death!
The deed is done:—Hail, king of Scotland, hail!
I see no more;—to many a fearful sound
The bloody cauldron sinks, and all is dark around.

Pity! touch the trembling strings,
A maid, a beauteous maniac, wildly sings:
They laid him in the ground so cold,
Upon his breast the earth is thrown;
High is heaped the grassy mould,
Oh! he is dead and gone.
The winds of the winter blow o'er his cold breast,
But pleasant shall be his rest.

O sovereign Master! at whose sole command
We start with terror, or with pity weep;
Oh! where is now thy all-creating wand;
Buried ten thousand thousand fathoms deep!
The staff is broke, the powerful spell is fled,
And never earthly guest shall in thy circle tread.

ABBA THULE'S LAMENT FOR HIS SON PRINCE LE BOO

I climb the highest cliff; I hear the sound
Of dashing waves; I gaze intent around;
I mark the gray cope, and the hollowness
Of heaven, and the great sun, that comes to bless
The isles again; but my long-straining eye,
No speck, no shadow can, far off, descry,
That I might weep tears of delight, and say,
It is the bark that bore my child away!
Sun, that returnest bright, beneath whose eye
The worlds unknown, and out-stretched waters lie,
Dost thou behold him now! On some rude shore,
Around whose crags the cheerless billows roar,
Watching the unwearied surges doth he stand,
And think upon his father's distant land!
Or has his heart forgot, so far away,

These native woods, these rocks, and torrents gray,
The tall bananas whispering to the breeze,
The shores, the sound of these encircling seas,
Heard from his infant days, and the piled heap
Of holy stones, where his forefathers sleep!
Ah, me! till sunk by sorrow, I shall dwell
With them forgetful in the narrow cell,
Never shall time from my fond heart efface
His image; oft his shadow I shall trace
Upon the glimmering waters, when on high
The white moon wanders through the cloudless sky.
Oft in my silent cave, when to its fire
From the night's rushing tempest we retire,
I shall behold his form, his aspect bland;
I shall retrace his footsteps on the sand;
And, when the hollow-sounding surges swell,
Still think I listen to his echoing shell.
Would I had perished ere that hapless day,
When the tall vessel, in its trim array,
First rushed upon the sounding surge, and bore
My age's comfort from this sheltering shore!
I saw it spread its white wings to the wind,
Too soon it left these hills and woods behind,
Gazing, its course I followed till mine eye
No longer could its distant track descry;
Till on the confines of the billows hoar
A while it hung, and then was seen no more,
And only the blue hollow cope I spied,
And the long waste of waters tossing wide.
More mournful then each falling surge I heard,
Then dropt the stagnant tear upon my beard.
Methought the wild waves said, amidst their roar
At midnight, Thou shalt see thy son no more!
Now thrice twelve moons through the mid heavens have rolled
And many a dawn, and slow night, have I told:
And still as every weary day goes by,
A knot recording on my line I tie;
But never more, emerging from the main,
I see the stranger's bark approach again.
Has the fell storm o'erwhelmed him! Has its sweep
Buried the bounding vessel in the deep!
Is he cast bleeding on some desert plain!
Upon his father did he call in vain!
Have pitiless and bloody tribes defiled
The cold limbs of my brave, my beauteous child!
Oh! I shall never, never hear his voice;
The spring-time shall return, the isles rejoice,
But faint and weary I shall meet the morn,

And 'mid the cheering sunshine droop forlorn!
The joyous conch sounds in the high wood loud,
O'er all the beach now stream the busy crowd;
Fresh breezes stir the waving plantain grove;
The fisher carols in the winding cove;
And light canoes along the lucid tide
With painted shells and sparkling paddles glide.
I linger on the desert rock alone,
Heartless, and cry for thee, my son, my son.

SOUTHAMPTON WATER

Smooth went our boat upon the summer seas,
Leaving, for so it seemed, the world behind,
Its sounds of mingled uproar: we, reclined
Upon the sunny deck, heard but the breeze
That o'er us whispering passed, or idly played
With the lithe flag aloft. A woodland scene
On either side drew its slope line of green,
And hung the water's shining edge with shade.
Above the woods, Netley! thy ruins pale
Peered as we passed; and Vecta's azure hue
Beyond the misty castle met our view;
Where in mid channel hung the scarce seen sail.
So all was calm and sunshine as we went
Cheerily o'er the briny element.
Oh! were this little boat to us the world,
As thus we wandered far from sounds of care,
Circled by friends and gentle maidens fair,
Whilst morning airs the waving pennant curled;
How sweet were life's long voyage, till in peace
We gained that haven still, where all things cease!

Isle of Wight.
Kelshot Castle.

THE PHILANTHROPIC SOCIETY. INSCRIBED TO THE DUKE OF LEEDS

When Want, with wasted mien and haggard eye,
Retires in silence to her cell to die;
When o'er her child she hangs with speechless dread,
Faint and despairing of to-morrow's bread;
Who shall approach to bid the conflict cease,
And to her parting spirit whisper peace!

Who thee, poor infant, that with aspect bland
Dost stretch forth innocent thy helpless hand,
Shall pitying then protect, when thou art thrown
On the world's waste, unfriended and alone!
O hapless Infancy! if aught could move
The hardest heart to pity and to love
'Twere surely found in thee: dim passions mark
Stern manhood's brow, where age impresses dark
The stealing line of sorrow; but thine eye
Wears not distrust, or grief, or perfidy.
Though fortune's storms with dismal shadow lower,
Thy heart nor fears, nor feels the bitter shower;
Thy tear is soon forgotten; thou wilt weep,
And then the murmuring winds will hush thy sleep,
As 'twere with some sad music;—and thy smiles,
Unlike to those that cover cruel wiles,
Plead best thy speechless innocence, and lend
A charm might win the world to be thy friend.
But thou art oft abandoned in thy smiles,
And early vice thy easy heart beguiles.
Oh for some voice, that of the secret maze
Where the grim passions lurk, the winding ways
That lead to sin, and ruth, and deep lament,
Might haply warn thee, whilst yet innocent
And beauteous as the spring-time o'er the hills
Advancing, when each vale glad music fills!
Else lost and wandering, the benighted mind
No spot of rest again shall ever find;
Then the sweet smiles, that erst enchanting laid
Their magic beauty on thy look, shall fade;
Then the bird's warbled song no more shall cheer
With morning music thy delighted ear;
Fell thoughts and muttering passions shall awake,
And the fair rose the sullied cheek forsake!
As when still Autumn's gradual gloom is laid
Far o'er the fading forest's saddened shade,
A mournful gleam illumines the cold hill,
Yet palely wandering o'er the distant rill;
But when the hollow gust, slow rising, raves,
And high the pine on yon lone summit waves,
Each milder charm, like pictures of a dream,
Hath perished, mute the birds, and dark the stream!
Scuds the dreer sleet upon the whirlwind borne,
And scowls the landscape clouded and forlorn!
So fades, so perishes frail Virtue's hue;
Her last and lingering smile seems but to rue,
Like autumn, every summer beauty reft,
Till all is dark and to the winter left.

Yet spring, with living touch, shall paint again
The green-leaved forest, and the purple plain;
With mingling melody the woods shall ring,
The whispering breeze its long-lost incense fling:
But, Innocence! when once thy tender flower
The sickly taint has touched, where is the power
That shall bring back its fragrance, or restore
The tints of loveliness, that shine no more?
How then for thee, who pinest in life's gloom,
Abandoned child! can hope or virtue bloom!
For thee, exposed amid the desert drear,
Which no glad gales or vernal sunbeams cheer!
Though some there are, who lift their head sublime,
Nor heed the transient storms of fate or time;
Too oft, alas! beneath unfriendly skies,
The tender blossom shrinks its leaves, and dies!
Go, struggle with thy fate, pursue thy way;—
Though thou art poor, the world around is gay!
Thou hast no bread; but on thy aching sight
Proud luxury's pavilions glitter bright;
In thy cold ear the song of gladness swells,
Whilst vacant folly chimes her tinkling bells:
The careless crowd prolong their hollow glee,
Nor one relenting bosom thinks of thee.
Will not the indignant spirit then rebel,
And the dark tide of passions fearful swell!
Will not despight, perhaps, or bitter need,
Urge then thy temper to some direful deed!
Pale Guilt shall call thee to her ghastly band,
Or Murder welcome thee with reeking hand!
O wretched state, where our best feelings lie
Deep sunk in sullen, hopeless apathy!
Or wakeful cares, or gloomy terrors start,
And night and tempest mingle in the heart!
All mournful to the pensive sage's eye,
The monuments of human glory lie;
Fall'n palaces, crushed by the ruthless haste
Of time, and many an empire's silent waste,
Where, 'midst the vale of long-departed years,
The form of desolation dim appears,
Pointing to the wild plain with ruin spread,
The wrecks of age, and records of the dead!
But where a sight shall shuddering sorrow find,
Sad as the ruins of the human mind;—
As Man, by his GREAT MAKER raised sublime
Amid the universe, ordained to climb
The arduous height where Virtue sits serene;—
As Man, the high lord of this nether scene,

So fall'n, so lost!—his noblest boast destroyed,
His sweet affections left a piteous void!
But oh, sweet Charity! what sounds were those
That met the listening ear, soft as the close
Of distant music, when the hum of day
Is hushed, and dying gales the airs convey!
Come, hapless orphans, meek Compassion cried,
Where'er, unsheltered outcasts! ye abide
The bitter driving wind, the freezing sky,
The oppressor's scourge, the proud man's contumely;
Come, hapless orphans! ye who never saw
A tear of kindness shed on your cold straw;
Who never met with joy the morning light,
Or lisped your little prayer of peace at night;
Come, hapless orphans! nor, when youth should spring
Soaring aloft, as on an eagle's wing,
Shall ye forsaken on the ground be left,
Of hope, of virtue, and of peace bereft!
Far from the springtide gale, and joyous day,
In the deep caverns of Despair ye lay:
She, iron-hearted mother, never pressed
Your wasted forms with transport to her breast;
When none o'er all the world your 'plaint would hear,
She never kissed away the falling tear,
Or fondly smiled, forgetful, to behold
Some infant grace its early charm unfold.
She ne'er with mingling hopes and rising fears,
Sighed for the fortune of your future years:
Or saw you hand in hand rejoicing stray
Beneath the morning sun, on youth's delightful way.
But happier scenes invite, and fairer skies;
From your dark bed, children of woe, arise!
In caves where peace ne'er smiled, where joy ne'er came,
Where Friendship's eye ne'er glistened at the name
Of one she loved, where famine and despair
Sat silent 'mid the damp and lurid air,
The soothing voice is heard; a beam of light
Is cast upon their features, sunk and white;
With trembling joy they catch the stealing sound;
Their famished little ones come smiling round.
Sweet Infancy! whom all the world forsook,
Thou hast put on again thy cherub look:
Guilt, shrinking at the sight, in deep dismay
Flies cowering, and resigns his wonted prey.
But who is she, in garb of misery clad,
Yet of less vulgar mien? A look so sad
The mourning maniac wears, so wild, yet meek;
A beam of joy now wanders o'er her cheek,

The pale eye visiting; it leaves it soon,
As fade the dewy glances of the moon
Upon some wandering cloud, while slow the ray
Retires, and leaves more dark the heaven's wide way.
Lost mother, early doomed to guilt and shame,
Whose friends of youth now sigh not o'er thy name,
Heavy has sorrow fall'n upon thy head,
Yet think—one hope remains when thou art dead;
Thy houseless child, thy only little one,
Shall not look round, defenceless and alone,
For one to guide her youth;—nor with dismay
Each stranger's cold unfeeling look survey.
She shall not now be left a prey to shame,
Whilst slow disease preys on her faded frame;
Nor, when the bloom of Innocence is fled,
Thus fainting bow her unprotected head.
Oh, she shall live, and Piety and Truth,
The loveliest ornaments, shall grace her youth.
And should her eye with softest lustre shine,
And should she wear such smiles as once were thine,
The smiles of peace and virtue they shall prove,
Blessing the calm abode of faithful love.
For ye who thus, by pure compassion taught,
Have wept o'er human sorrows;—who have sought
Want's dismal cell, and pale as from the dead
To life and light the speechless orphan led;—
Trust that the deed, in Mercy's book enrolled,
Approving spirits of the just behold!
Meanwhile, new virtues here, as on the wing
Of morn, from Sorrow's dreary shades shall spring;
Young Modesty, with fair untainted bloom;
And Industry, that sings beside her loom;
And ruddy Labour, issuing from his hatch
Ere the slant sunbeam strikes the lowly thatch;
And sweet Contentment, smiling on a rock,
Like a fair shepherdess beside her flock;
And tender Love, that hastes with myrtle-braid
To bind the tresses of the favoured maid;
And Piety, with unclasped holy book,
Lifting to heaven her mildly-beaming look:
These village virtues on the plain shall throng,
And Albion's hills resound a cheerful song;
Whilst Charity, with dewy eyelids bland,
Leading a lisping infant in her hand,
Shall bend at pure Religion's holy shrine,
And say, These children, GOD OF LOVE, are thine!

THE DYING SLAVE

Faint-gazing on the burning orb of day,
When Afric's injured son expiring lay,
His forehead cold, his labouring bosom bare,
His dewy temples, and his sable hair,
His poor companions kissed, and cried aloud,
Rejoicing, whilst his head in peace he bowed:—
Now thy long, long task is done,
Swiftly, brother, wilt thou run,
Ere to-morrow's golden beam
Glitter on thy parent stream,
Swiftly the delights to share,
The feast of joy that waits thee there.
Swiftly, brother, wilt thou ride
O'er the long and stormy tide,
Fleeter than the hurricane,
Till thou see'st those scenes again,
Where thy father's hut was reared,
Where thy mother's voice was heard;
Where thy infant brothers played
Beneath the fragrant citron shade;
Where through green savannahs wide
Cooling rivers silent glide,
Or the shrill cicalas sing
Ceaseless to their murmuring;
Where the dance, the festive song,
Of many a friend divided long,
Doomed through stranger lands to roam,
Shall bid thy spirit welcome home!
Fearless o'er the foaming tide
Again thy light canoe shall ride;
Fearless on the embattled plain
Thou shalt lift thy lance again;
Or, starting at the call of morn,
Wake the wild woods with thy horn;
Or, rushing down the mountain-slope,
O'ertake the nimble antelope;
Or lead the dance, 'mid blissful bands,
On cool Andracte's yellow sands;
Or, in the embowering orange-grove,
Tell to thy long-forsaken love
The wounds, the agony severe,
Thy patient spirit suffered here!
Fear not now the tyrant's power,
Past is his insulting hour;
Mark no more the sullen trait

On slavery's brow of scorn and hate;
Hear no more the long sigh borne
Murmuring on the gales of morn!
Go in peace; yet we remain
Far distant toiling on in pain;
Ere the great Sun fire the skies
To our work of woe we rise;
And see each night, without a friend,
The world's great comforter descend!
Tell our brethren, where ye meet,
Thus we toil with weary feet;
Yet tell them that Love's generous flame,
In joy, in wretchedness the same,
In distant worlds was ne'er forgot;
And tell them that we murmur not;
Tell them, though the pang will start,
And drain the life-blood from the heart,—
Tell them, generous shame forbids
The tear to stain our burning lids!
Tell them, in weariness and want,
For our native hills we pant,
Where soon, from shame and sorrow free,
We hope in death to follow thee!

SONG OF THE AMERICAN INDIAN

Stranger, stay, nor wish to climb
The heights of yonder hills sublime;
For there strange shapes and spirits dwell,
That oft the murmuring thunders swell,
Of power from the impending steep
To hurl thee headlong to the deep;
But secure with us abide,
By the winding river's side;
Our gladsome toil, our pleasures share,
And think not of a world of care.
The lonely cayman, where he feeds
Among the green high-bending reeds,
Shall yield thee pastime; thy keen dart
Through his bright scales shall pierce his heart.
Home returning from our toils,
Thou shalt bear the tiger's spoils;
And we will sing our loudest strain
O'er the forest-tyrant slain!
Sometimes thou shalt pause to hear
The beauteous cardinal sing clear;

Where hoary oaks, by time decayed,
Nod in the deep wood's pathless glade;
And the sun, with bursting ray,
Quivers on the branches gray.
By the river's craggy banks,
O'erhung with stately cypress-ranks,
Where the bush-bee hums his song,
Thy trim canoe shall glance along.
To-night at least, in this retreat,
Stranger! rest thy wandering feet;
To-morrow, with unerring bow,
To the deep thickets fearless we will go.

MONODY, WRITTEN AT MATLOCK

Matlock! amid thy hoary-hanging views,
Thy glens that smile sequestered, and thy nooks
Which yon forsaken crag all dark o'erlooks;
Once more I court the long neglected Muse,
As erst when by the mossy brink and falls
Of solitary Wainsbeck, or the side
Of Clysdale's cliffs, where first her voice she tried,
I strayed a pensive boy. Since then, the thralls
That wait life's upland road have chilled her breast,
And much, as much they might, her wing depressed.
Wan Indolence, resigned, her deadening hand
Laid on her heart, and Fancy her cold wand
Dropped at the frown of fortune; yet once more
I call her, and once more her converse sweet,
'Mid the still limits of this wild retreat,
I woo;—if yet delightful as of yore
My heart she may revisit, nor deny
The soothing aid of some sweet melody!
I hail the rugged scene that bursts around;
I mark the wreathed roots, the saplings gray,
That bend o'er the dark Derwent's wandering way;
I mark its stream with peace-persuading sound,
That steals beneath the fading foliage pale,
Or, at the foot of frowning crags upreared,
Complains like one forsaken and unheard.
To me, it seems to tell the pensive tale
Of spring-time, and the summer days all flown;
And while sad autumn's voice ev'n now I hear
Along the umbrage of the high-wood moan,
At intervals, whose shivering leaves fall sere;
Whilst o'er the group of pendant groves I view

The slowly-spreading tints of pining hue,
I think of poor Humanity's brief day,
How fast its blossoms fade, its summers speed away!
When first young Hope, a golden-tressed boy,
Most musical his early madrigal
Sings to the whispering waters as they fall,
Breathing fresh airs of fragrance and of joy,
The wild woods gently wave, the morning sheds
Her rising radiance on the mountain heads,
Strewed with green isles appears old ocean's reign,
And seen at distance rays of resting light
Silver the farthest promontory's height:
Then hushed is the long murmur of the main,
Whilst silent o'er the slowly-crisping tides,
Bound to some beaming spot, the bark of pleasure glides.
Alas! the scenes that smile in light arrayed
But catch the sense, and then in darkness fade.
We, poor adventurers, of peace bereft,
Look back on the green hills that late we left,
Or turn, with beating breast and anxious eye,
To some faint hope that glimmering meets our sight
(Like the lone watch-tower in the storm of night),
Then on the dismal waste are driv'n despairing by!
Meantime, amid the landscape cold and mute,
Hope, sweet enchanter, sighing drops his lute:
So sad decay and mortal change succeeds,
And o'er the silent scene Time, like a giant, speeds!
Yet the bleak cliffs that lift their heads so high
(Around whose beetling crags, with ceaseless coil,
And still-returning flight, the ravens toil)
Heed not the changeful seasons as they fly,
Nor spring, nor autumn: they their hoary brow
Uprear, and ages past, as in this now,
The same deep trenches unsubdued have worn,
The same majestic frown, and looks of lofty scorn.
So Fortitude, a mailed warrior old,
Appears; he lifts his scar-intrenched crest;
The tempest gathers round his dauntless breast;
He hears far off the storm of havoc rolled;
The feeble fall around: their sound is past;
Their sun is set, their place no more is known;
Like the wan leaves before the winter's blast
They perish:—He, unshaken and alone
Remains, his brow a sterner shade assumes,
By age ennobled, whilst the hurricane,
That raves resistless o'er the ravaged plain,
But shakes unfelt his helmet's quivering plume.
And so yon sovereign of the scene I mark

Above the woods rear his majestic head,
That soon all shattered at his feet shall shed
Their short-lived beauties: he the winter dark
Regardless, and the wasteful time that flies,
Rejoicing in his lonely might, defies.
Thee, wandering in the deep and craggy dell,
Sequestered stream, with other thoughts I view:
Thou dost in solitude thy course pursue,
As thou hadst bid life's busy scenes farewell,
Yet making still such music as might cheer
The weary passenger that journeys near.
Such are the songs of Peace in Virtue's shade;
Unheard of Folly, or the vacant train
That pipe and dance upon the noontide plain,
Till in the dust together they are laid!
But not unheard of Him, who sits sublime
Above the clouds of this tempestuous clime,
Its stir and strife; to whom more grateful rise
The humble incense, and the still small voice
Of those that on their pensive way rejoice,
Than shouts of thousands echoing to the skies;
Than songs of conquest pealing round the car
Of hard Ambition, or the Fiend of War,
Sated with slaughter. Nor may I, sweet stream,
From thy wild banks and still retreats depart,
Where now I meditate my casual theme,
Without some mild improvement on my heart
Poured sad, yet pleasing! so may I forget
The crosses and the cares that sometimes fret
Life's smoothest channel, and each wish prevent
That mars the silent current of content!
In such a spot, amidst these rugged views,
The pensive poet in his drooping age
Might wish to place his reed-roofed hermitage;
Where much on life's vain shadows he might muse.
If fortune smiled not on his early way,
If he were doomed to mourn a faithless friend,
Here he might rest, and when his hairs were gray,
Behold in peace the parting day descend.
If a hard world his errors scanned severe,
When late the earth received his mouldering clay,
Perhaps some loved companion, wandering near,
Plucking the gray moss from the stone, might say:
Him I remember, in our careless days,
Vacant and glad, till many a loss severe
First hung his placid eyelids with a tear;
Yet on such visions ardent would he gaze,
As the Muse loved, that oft would smile and die,

Like the faint bow that leaves the weeping sky;
His heart unguarded, yet it proudly beat
Against hard wrong, or coward cold deceit;—
Nor passed he e'er without a sigh the cell
Where wretchedness and her pale children dwell.
He never wished to win the world's cold ear,
Nor, prized by those he loved, its blame could fear;
Its praise he left to those who, at their will,
The ingenious strain of torturing art could trill!
Content, as random fancies might inspire,
If his weak reed, at times, or plaintive lyre,
He touched with desultory hand, and drew
Some softened tones, to Nature not untrue.
The leaves, O Derwent! on thy bosom still
Oft with the gust now fall—the season pale
Hath smote with hand unseen the silent vale,
And slowly steals the verdure from the hill;
So the fair scene departs, yet wears a while
The lingering traces of its beauteous smile:
But we who by thy margin stray, or climb
The cliff's aërial height, or join the song
Of hope and gladness amidst yonder throng,
Losing the brief and fleeting hours of time,
Reck not how age, even thus, with icy hand,
Hangs o'er us;—how, as with a wizard's wand,
Youth blooming like the spring, and roseate mirth,
To slow and sere consumption he shall change,
And with invisible mutation strange,
Withered and wasted send them to the earth;
Whilst hushed, and by the mace of ruin rent,
Sinks the forsaken hall of merriment!
Bright bursts the sun upon the shaggy scene!
The aged rocks their glittering summits gray
Hang beautiful amid the beams of day;
And all the woods, with slowly-fading green,
Yet smiling wave:—severer thoughts, away!
The night is distant, and the lovely day
Looks on us yet;—the sound of mirthful cheer
From yonder dome comes pleasant to mine ear.
From rock to rock reverberated swells,
Hark,—the glad music of the village bells!
On the crag's naked point the heifer lows,
And wide below the brightening landscape glows!
Though brief the time and short our course to run,
Derwent! amid the scenes that deck thy side,
Ere yet the parting paths of life divide,
Let us rejoice, seeking what may be won
From the laborious day, or fortune's frown:

Here may we, ere the sun of life goes down,
A while regardless of the morrow, dwell;
Then to our destined roads, and speed us well!

THE RIGHT HONOURABLE EDMUND BURKE

Why mourns the ingenuous Moralist, whose mind
Science has stored, and Piety refined,
That fading Chivalry displays no more
Her pomp and stately tournaments of yore!
Lo! when Philosophy and Truth advance,
Scared at their frown, she drops her glittering lance;
Round her reft castles the pale ivy crawls,
And sunk and silent are her bannered halls!
As when far off the golden evening sails,
And slowly sink the fancy-painted vales,
With rich pavilions spread in long array;
So rolls the enchanter's radiant realm away;
So on the sight the parting glories fade,
The gorgeous vision sets in endless shade.
But shall the musing mind for this lament,
Or mourn the wizard's Gothic fabric rent!
Shall he, with Fancy's poor and pensive child,
Gaze on his shadowy vales, and prospects wild,
With lingering love, and sighing bid farewell
To the dim pictures of his parting spell!
No, BURKE! thy heart, by juster feelings led,
Mourns for the spirit of high Honour fled;
Mourns that Philosophy, abstract and cold,
Withering should smite life's fancy-flowered mould;
And many a smiling sympathy depart,
That graced the sternness of the manly heart.
Nor shall the wise and virtuous scan severe
These fair illusions, ev'n to nature dear.
Though now no more proud Chivalry recalls
Her tourneys bright, and pealing festivals;
Though now on high her idle spear is hung,
Though Time her mouldering harp has half unstrung;
Her milder influence shall she still impart,
To decorate, but not disguise, the heart;
To nurse the tender sympathies that play
In the short sunshine of life's early way;
For female worth and meekness to inspire
Homage and love, and temper rude desire;
Nor seldom with sweet dreams sad thoughts to cheer,
And half beguile affliction of her tear!

Lo! this her boast; and still, O BURKE! be thine
Her glowing hues that warm, yet tempered shine;
Whilst whispers bland, and fairest dreams, attend
Thy evening path, till the last shade descend!
So may she soothe, with loftier wisdom's aid,
Thy musing leisure in the silent shade,
And bid poor Fancy, her cold pinions wet,
Life's cloudy skies and beating showers forget.
But can her fairest form, her sweetest song,
Soothe thee, assailed by calumny and wrong!
Ev'n now thy foes with louder accents cry:
Champion of unrelenting tyranny,
At Freedom hast thou aimed the deadly blow,
And striven with impious arm to lay her altars low!
No, BURKE! indignant at the voice we start:
We trust thy liberal views, thy generous heart;
We think of those who, naked, pale, and poor,
Relieved and blessed, have wandered from thy door;
We see thee with unwearied step explore
Each track of bloodshed on the farthest shore
Of injured Asia, and thy swelling breast
Harrowing the oppressor, mourning for the oppressed,
No, BURKE! where'er Injustice rears her head,
Where'er with blood her idol grim is fed;
Where'er fell Cruelty, at her command,
With crimson banner marches through the land,
And striding, like a giant, onward hies,
Whilst man, a trodden worm, looks up, and dies;
Where'er pale Murder in her train appears,
With reeking axe, and garments wet with tears;
Or, lowering Jealousy, unmoved as Fate,
Bars fast the prison-cage's iron gate
Upon the buried sorrows and the cries
Of him who there, lost and forgotten, lies;—
When ministers like these, in fearful state,
Upon a bloody tyrant's bidding wait,
Thou too shalt own (and Justice lift her rod)
The cause of Freedom is the cause of GOD!
Fair spirit, who dost rise in beauteous pride,
Where proud Oppression hath thine arm defied!
When led by Virtue thou dost firm advance,
And bathe in Guilt's warm blood thy burning lance;
When all thy form its awful port assumes,
And in the tempest shake thy crimson plumes,
I mark thy lofty mien, thy steady eye,
So fall thy foes! with tears of joy I cry.
But ne'er may Anarchy, with eyes a-flame,
And mien distract, assume thy awful name;

Her pale torch sheds afar its hideous glare,
And shows the blood-drops in her dabbled hair;
The fiends of discord hear her hollow voice,
The spirits of the deathful storm rejoice:
As when the rising blast with muttering sweep
Sounds 'mid the branches of the forest deep,
The sad horizon lowers, the parting sun
Is hid, strange murmurs through the high wood run,
The falcon wheels away his mournful flight,
And leaves the glens to solitude and night;
Till soon the hurricane, in dismal shroud,
Comes fearful forth, and sounds her conch aloud;
The oak majestic bows his hoary head,
And ruin round his ancient reign is spread:
So the dark fiend, rejoicing in her might,
Pours desolation and the storm of night;
Before her dread career the good and just
Fly far, or sink expiring in the dust;
Wide wastes and mighty wrecks around her lie,
And the earth trembles at her impious cry!
Whether her temple, wet with human gore,
She thus may raise on Gallia's ravaged shore,
Belongs to HIM alone, and His high will,
Who bids the tempests of the world be still.
With joy we turn to Albion's happier plain,
Where ancient Freedom holds her temperate reign;
Where Justice sits majestic on her throne;
Where Mercy turns her ear to every groan.
O Albion! fairest isle, whose verdant plain
Springs beauteous from the blue and billowy main;
In peaceful pomp whose glittering cities rise,
And lift their crowded temples to the skies;
Whose navy on the broad brine awful rolls;
Whose commerce glows beneath the distant poles;
Whose streams reflect full many an Attic pile;
Whose velvet lawns in long luxuriance smile;
Amid whose winding coombs contentment dwells,
Whose vales rejoice to hear the Sabbath bells;
Whose humblest shed, that steady laws protect,
The villager with woodbine bowers hath decked!
Sweet native land, whose every haunt is dear,
Whose every gale is music to mine ear;
Amidst whose hills one poor retreat I sought,
Where I might sometimes hide a saddening thought,
And having wandered far, and marked mankind
In their vain mask, might rest and safety find:
Oh! still may Freedom, with majestic mien,
Pacing thy rocks and the green vales, be seen;

Around thy cliffs, that glitter o'er the main,
May smiling Order wind her silver chain;
Whilst from thy calm abodes, and azure skies,
Far off the fiend of Discord murmuring flies!
To him who firm thy injured cause has fought,
This humble offering, lo! the Muse has brought;
Nor heed thou, BURKE, if, with averted eye,
Scowling, cold Envy may thy worth decry!
It is the lot of man:—the best oft mourn,
As sad they journey through this cloudy bourne:
If conscious Genius stamp their chosen breast,
And on the forehead show her seal impressed,
Perhaps they mourn, in bleak Misfortune's shade,
Their age and cares with penury repaid;
Their errors deeply scanned, their worth forgot,
Or marked by hard injustice with a blot.
If high they soar, and keep their distant way,
And spread their ample pinions to the day,
Malignant Faction hears with hate their name,
And all her tongues are busy with their fame.
But 'tis enough to hold, as best we may,
Our destined track, till sets the closing day;
Whether with living lustre we adorn
Our high sphere, like the radiance of the morn;
Or whether silent in the shade we move,
Cheered by the lonely star of pensive love;
Or whether wild opposing storms we stem,
Panting for Virtue's distant diadem;
'Tis the unshaken mind, the conscience pure,
That bids us firmly act, meekly endure;
'Tis this may shield us when the storm beats hard,
Content, though poor, had we no other guard!

ON LEAVING A PLACE OF RESIDENCE

If I could bid thee, pleasant shade, farewell
Without a sigh, amidst whose circling bowers
My stripling prime was passed, and happiest hours,
Dead were I to the sympathies that swell
The human breast! These woods, that whispering wave,
My father reared and nursed, now to the grave
Gone down; he loved their peaceful shades, and said,
Perhaps, as here he mused: Live, laurels green;
Ye pines that shade the solitary scene,
Live blooming and rejoice! When I am dead
My son shall guard you, and amid your bowers,

Like me, find shelter from life's beating showers.
These thoughts, my father, every spot endear;
And whilst I think, with self-accusing pain,
A stranger shall possess the loved domain,
In each low wind I seem thy voice to hear.
But these are shadows of the shaping brain
That now my heart, alas! can ill sustain:
We must forget—the world is wide—the abode
Of peace may still be found, nor hard the road.
It boots not, so, to every chance resigned,
Where'er the spot, we bear the unaltered mind.
Yet, oh! poor cottage, and thou sylvan shade,
Remember, ere I left your coverts green,
Where in my youth I mused, in childhood played,
I gazed, I paused, I dropped a tear unseen,
That bitter from the font of memory fell,
Thinking on him who reared you; now, farewell!

ELEGIAC STANZAS

WRITTEN DURING SICKNESS AT BATH

When I lie musing on my bed alone,
And listen to the wintry waterfall;
And many moments that are past and gone,
Moments of sunshine and of joy, recall;

Though the long night is dark and damp around,
And no still star hangs out its friendly flame;
And the winds sweep the sash with sullen sound,
And freezing palsy creeps o'er all my frame;

I catch consoling phantasies that spring
From the thick gloom, and as the night airs beat,
They touch my heart, like wind-swift wires that ring
In mournful modulations, strange and sweet.

Was it the voice of thee, my buried friend?
Was it the whispered vow of faithful love?
Do I in Knoyle's green shades thy steps attend,
And hear the high pines murmur thus above?

'Twas not thy voice, my buried friend!—Oh, no:
'Twas not, O Knoyle! the murmur of thy trees;
But at the thought I feel my bosom glow,
And woo the dream whose air-drawn shadows please.

And I can think I see the groves again,
The larches that yon peaceful roof embower;
The airy down, the cattle-speckled plain,
And the slant sunshine on the village tower.

And I can think I hear its Sabbath chime
Come smoothly softened down the woody vale;
Or mark on yon lone eminence sublime,
Fast whirling in the wind, the white mill's sail.

Phantom, that by my bed dost beckoning glide,
Spectre of Death, to the damp charnel hie!
Thy dim pale hand, thy festering visage hide;
Thou com'st to say, I with thy worms shall lie!

Thou com'st to say that my once vacant mind
Amid those scenes shall never more rejoice;
Nor on the day of rest the hoary hind
Bend o'er his staff, attentive to my voice.

Hast thou not visited that pleasant place
Where in this hard world I have happiest been?
And shall I tremble at thy lifted mace
That hath pierced all on which life seemed to lean?

But Hope might whisper: Many a smiling day
And many a cheerful eve may yet be mine,
Ere age's autumn strew my locks with gray,
And weary to the dust my steps decline.

I argue not, but uncomplaining bow
To Heaven's high 'hest; secure, whate'er my lot,
Meek spirit of resigned Content, that thou
Wilt smooth my pillow, and forsake me not!

Thou to the turfy hut with pilgrim feet
Wanderest, from halls of loud tumultuous joy;
Or on the naked down, when the winds beat,
Dost sing to the forsaken shepherd boy.

Thou art the sick man's nurse, the poor man's friend,
And through each change of life thou hast been mine;
In every ill thou canst a comfort blend,
And bid the eye, though sad, in sadness shine.

Thee I have met on Cherwell's willowed side,
And when our destined road far onward lay,

Thee I have found, whatever chance betide,
The kind companion of my devious way.

With thee unwearied have I loved to roam,
By the smooth-flowing Scheldt, or rushing Rhine;
And thou hast gladdened my sequestered home,
And hung my peaceful porch with eglantine.

When cares and crosses my tired spirits tried,
When to the dust my father I resigned;
Amidst the quiet shade unseen I sighed,
And, blest with thee, forgot a world unkind.

Ev'n now, while toiling through the sleepless night,
A tearful look to distant scenes I cast,
And the glad objects that once charmed my sight
Remember, like soft views of "faerie" past;

I see thee come half-smiling to my bed,
With Fortitude more awfully severe,
Whose arm sustaining holds my drooping head,
Who dries with her dark locks the tender tear.

O firmer Spirit! on some craggy height
Who, when the tempest sails aloft, dost stand,
And hear'st the ceaseless billows of the night
Rolling upon the solitary strand;

At this sad hour, when no harsh thoughts intrude
To mar the melancholy mind's repose,
When I am left to night and solitude,
And languid life seems verging to its close;

Oh, let me thy pervading influence feel;
Be every weak and wayward thought repressed;
And hide thou, as with plates of coldest steel,
The faded aspect and the throbbing breast!

Silent the motley pageant may retreat,
And vain mortality's brief scenes remove;
Yet let my bosom, whilst with life it beat,
Breathe a last prayer for all on earth I love.

Slow-creeping pain weighs down my heavy eye,
A chiller faintness steals upon my breast;
"O gentle Muse, with some sweet lullaby"
Rock me in long forgetfulness to rest!

ON LEAVING WINCHESTER SCHOOL

The spring shall visit thee again,
Itchin! and yonder ancient fane,
That casts its shadow on thy breast,
As if, by many winters beat,
The blooming season it would greet,
With many a straggling wild-flower shall be dressed.

But I, amid the youthful train
That stray at evening by thy side,
No longer shall a guest remain,
To mark the spring's reviving pride.
I go not unrejoicing; but who knows,
When I have shared, O world! thy common woes,
Returning I may drop some natural tears;
As these same fields I look around,
And hear from yonder dome the slow bell sound,
And think upon the joys that crowned my stripling years!

HOPE, AN ALLEGORICAL SKETCH

But thou, O Hope! with eyes so fair,
What was thy delightful measure?
COLLINS.

I am the comforter of them that mourn;
My scenes well shadowed, and my carol sweet,
Cheer the poor passengers of life's rude bourne,
Till they are sheltered in that last retreat,
Where human toils and troubles are forgot.
These sounds I heard amid this mortal road,
When I had reached with pain one pleasant spot,
So that for joy some tears in silence flowed;
I raised mine eyes, sickness had long depressed,
And felt thy warmth, O sun! come cheering to my breast.

The storm of night had ceased upon the plain,
When thoughtful in the forest-walk I strayed,
To the long hollow murmur of the main
Listening, and to the many leaves that made
A drowsy cadence, as the high trees waved;
When straight a beauteous scene burst on my sight;
Smooth were the waters that the lowland laved:

And lo! a form, as of some fairy sprite,
Who held in her right hand a budding spray,
And like a sea-maid sung her sweetly warbled lay.

Soothing as steals the summer-wave she sung:
The grisly phantoms of the night are gone
To hear in shades forlorn the death-bell rung;
But thou whom sickness hast left weak and wan,
Turn from their spectre-terrors the green sea
That whispers at my feet, the matin gale
That crisps its shining marge shall solace thee,
And thou my long-forgotten voice shalt hail,
For I am Hope, whom weary hearts confess
The soothest sprite that sings on life's long wilderness.

As slowly ceased her tender voice, I stood
Delighted: the hard way, so lately passed,
Seemed smooth; the ocean's bright extended flood
Before me stretched; the clouds that overcast
Heaven's melancholy vault hurried away,
Driven seaward, and the azure hills appeared;
The sunbeams shone upon their summits gray,
Strange saddening sounds no more by fits were heard,
But birds, in new leaves shrouded, sung aloft,
And o'er the level seas Spring's healing airs blew soft.

As when a traveller, who many days
Hath journeyed 'mid Arabian deserts still,
A dreary solitude far on surveys,
And met, nor flitting bird, nor gushing rill,
But near some marble ruin, gleaming pale,
Sighs mindful of the haunts of cheerful man,
And thinks he hears in every sickly gale
The bells of some approaching caravan;
At length, emerging o'er the dim tract, sees
Damascus' golden fanes, and minarets, and trees:

So beat my bosom when my winding way
Led through the thickets to a sheltered vale,
Where the fair syren sat; a smooth clear bay
Skirted with woods appeared, where many a sail
Went shining o'er the watery surface still,
Lessening at last in the gray ocean flood;
And yonder, half-way up the fronting hill,
Peeping from forth the trees, a cottage stood,
Above whose peaceful umbrage, trailing high,
A little smoke went up, and stained the cloudless sky.

I turned, and lo! a mountain seemed to rise,
Upon whose top a spiry citadel
Lifted its dim-seen turrets to the skies,
Where some high lord of the domain might dwell;
And onward, where the eye scarce stretched its sight,
Hills over hills in long succession rose,
Touched with a softer and yet softer light,
And all was blended as in deep repose;
The woods, the sea, the hills that shone so fair,
Till woods, and sea, and hills seemed fading into air.

At once, methought, I saw a various throng
To this enchanting spot their footsteps bend;
All drawn, sweet Hope! by thy inspiring song,
Which melodies scarce mortal seem to blend.
First buxom Youth, with cheeks of glowing red,
Came lightly tripping o'er the morning dew,
He wore a harebell garland on his head,
And stretched his hands at the bright-bursting view:
A mountain fawn went bounding by his side,
Around whose slender neck a silver bell was tied.

Then said I: Mistress of the magic song,
Oh, pity 'twere that hearts that know no guile
Should ever feel the pangs of truth or wrong!
She heeded not, but sang with lovelier smile:
Enjoy, O youth, the season of thy May;
Hark, how the throstles in the hawthorn sing!
The hoary Time, that resteth night nor day,
O'er the earth's shade may speed with noiseless wing;
But heed not thou; snatch the brief joys that rise,
And sport beneath the light of these unclouded skies.

His fine eye flashing an unwonted fire,
Then Fancy o'er the glade delighted went;
He struck at times a small and silver lyre,
Or gazed upon the rolling element;
Sometimes he took his mirror, which did show
The various landscape lovelier than the life;
Beaming more bright the vivid tints did glow,
And so well mingled was the colours' strife,
That the fond heart, the beauteous shades once seen,
Would sigh for such retreats, for vales and woods so green!

Gay was his aspect, and his airy vest,
As loose it flowed, such colours did display,
As paint the clouds reposing in the west,
Or the moist rainbow's radiant arch inlay;

And now he tripped, like fairy of the wood,
And seemed with dancing spirits to rejoice,
And now he hung his head in pensive mood:
Meantime, O Hope! he listened to thy voice,
And whilst of joy and youth it cheerly sung,
He touched his answering harp, and o'er the valley sprung.

Pleasure, a frolic nymph, to the glad sound
Came dancing, as all tears she might forget;
And now she gazed with a sweet archness round,
And wantonly displayed a silken net:
She won her way with fascinating air—
Her eyes illumined with a tender light,
Her smile's strange blandishment, her shaded hair
That lengthening hung, her teeth as ivory white,
That peeped from her moist lip, seemed to inspire
Tumultuous wishes warm, and dreams of fond desire.

What softer passions did thy bosom move,
When those melodious measures met thine ear,
Child of Sincerity, and virtuous Love!
Thine eyes did shine beneath a blissful tear
That still were turned towards the tranquil scene,
Where the thin smoke rose from the embowered cot;
And thou didst think, that there, with smile serene,
In quiet shades, and every pang forgot,
Thou mightest sink on pure Affection's breast,
And listen to the winds that whispered thee to rest.

I thought, O Love, how seldom art thou found
Without annoyance in this earthly state!
For, haply, thou dost feed some rankling wound,
Or on thy youth pale poverty doth wait,
Till years, on heavy wing, have rolled away;
Or where thou most didst hope firm faith to see,
Thou meetest fickleness estranged and cold;
Or if some true and tender heart there be,
On which, through every change, thy soul might trust,
Death comes with his fell dart, and smites it to the dust!

But lusty Enterprise, with looks of glee,
Approached the drooping youth, as he would say,
Come to the high woods and the hills with me,
And cast thy sullen myrtle-wreath away.
Upon a neighing courser he did sit,
That stretched its arched neck, in conscious pride,
And champed as with disdain a golden bit,
But Hope her animating voice applied,

And Enterprise with speed impetuous passed,
Whilst the long vale returned his wreathed bugle's blast.

Suddenly, lifting high his ponderous spear,
A mailed man came forth with scornful pride,
I saw him, towering in his proud career,
Along the valley with a giant stride:
Upon his helm, in letters of bright gold,
That to the sun's meridian splendour shone,
Ambition's name far off I might behold.
Meantime from earth there came a hollow moan;
But Fame, who followed, her loud trumpet blew,
And to the murmuring beach with eyes a-flame he flew.

And now already had he gained the strand,
Where a tall vessel rode with sail unfurled,
And soon he thought to reach the farther land,
Which to his eager eye seemed like a world
That he by strength might win and make his own;
And in that citadel, which shone so bright,
Seat him, a purple sovereign, on his throne.
So he went tilting o'er the waters white,
And whilst he oft looked back with stern disdain,
In louder tone, methought, was heard the inspiring strain:

By the shade of cities old,
By many a river stained with gore,
By the sword of Sesac bold,
Who smote the nations from the shore
Of ancient Nile to India's farthest plain,
By Fame's proud pillars, and by Valour's shield
By mighty chiefs in glorious battle slain,
Assert thy sway; amid the bloody field
Pursue thy march, and to the heights sublime
Of Honour's glittering cliffs, a mighty conqueror climb!

Then said I, in my heart: Man, thou dost rear
Thine eye to heaven, and vaunt thy lofty worth;
The ensign of dominion thou dost bear
O'er nature's works; but thou dost oft go forth,
Urged by proud hopes to ravage and destroy,
Thou dost build up a name by cruel deeds;
Whilst to the peaceful scenes of love and joy,
Sorrow, and crime, and solitude, succeeds.
Hence, when her war-song Victory doth sing,
Destruction flaps aloft her iron-hurtling wing.

But see, as one awakened from a trance,

With hollow and dim eyes and stony stare,
Captivity with faltering step advance!
Dripping and knotted was her coal-black hair;
For she had long been hid, as in the grave;
No sounds the silence of her prison broke,
Nor one companion had she in her cave,
Save Terror's dismal shape, that no word spoke;
But to a stony coffin on the floor
With lean and hideous finger pointed evermore.

The lark's shrill song, the early village chime,
The upland echo of the winding horn,
The far-heard clock that spoke the passing time,
Had never pierced her solitude forlorn;
At length, released from the deep dungeon's gloom,
She feels the fragrance of the vernal gale;
She sees more sweet the living landscape bloom,
And while she listens to Hope's tender tale,
She thinks her long-lost friends shall bless her sight,
And almost faints with joy amid the broad daylight.

And near the spot, as with reluctant feet,
Slowly desponding Melancholy drew,
The wind and rain her naked breast had beat,
Sunk was her eye, and sallow was her hue:
In the huge forest's unrejoicing shade
Bewildered had she wandered day by day,
And many a grisly fiend her heart dismayed,
And cold and wet upon the ground she lay;
But now such sounds with mellow sweetness stole,
As lapped in dreams of bliss her slow-consenting soul.

Next, to the woody glen poor Mania strayed,
Most pale and wild, yet gentle was her look;
A slender garland she of straw had made,
Of flowers and rushes from the running brook;
But as she sadly passed, the tender sound
Of its sharp pang her wounded heart beguiled;
She dropped her half-made garland on the ground,
And then she sighed, and then in tears she smiled:
But in such sort, that Pity would have said,
O GOD, be merciful to that poor hapless maid!

Now ravingly she cried: The whelming main—
The wintry wave rolls over his cold head;
I never shall behold his form again;
Hence flattering fancies—he is dead, is dead!
Perhaps on some wild shore he may be cast,

Where on their prey barbarians howling rush,
Oh, fiercer they, than is the whelming blast!
Hush, my poor heart! my wakeful sorrows, hush!
He lives! I yet shall press him to my heart,
And cry, Oh no, no, no,—we never more will part!

So sang she, when despairing, from his cell,
Hid furthest in the lone umbrageous wood,
Where many a winter he had loved to dwell,
Came grim Remorse; fixed in deep thought he stood,
His senses pierced by the unwonted tone;
Some stagnant blood-drops from his locks he shook;
He saw the trees that waved, the sun that shone,
He cast around an agonised look;
Then with a ghastly smile, that spoke his pain,
He hied him to his cave in thickest shades again.

And now the sun sank westward, and the sky
Was hung with thousand lucid pictures gay;
When gazing on the scenec with placid eye,
An ancient man appeared in amice gray;
His sandal shoes were by long travel worn,
O'er hill and valley, many a weary mile,
Yet drooped he not, like one in years forlorn;
His pale cheek wore a sad, but tender smile;
'Twas sage Experience, by his look confessed,
And white as frost his beard descended to his breast.

Thus said I: Master, pleasant is this place,
And sweet are those melodious notes I hear,
And happy they among man's toiling race
Who, of their cares forgetful, wander near;
Me they delight, whom sickness and slow pain
Have bowed almost to death with heavy hand;
The fairy scenes refresh my heart again,
And, pleased, I listen to that music bland,
Which seems to promise hours of joy to come,
And bids me tranquil seek my poor but peaceful home.

He said: Alas! these shadows soon may fly,
Like the gay creatures of the element;
Yet do poor mortals still with raptured eye
Behold like thee the pictures they present;
And, charmed by Hope's sweet music, on they fare,
And think they soon shall reach that blissful goal,
Where never more the sullen knell of Care
For buried friends and severed loves shall toll:
So on they fare, till all their troubles cease,

And on a lap of earth they lie them down in peace.

But not there ceases their immortal claim;
From golden clouds I heard a small voice say:
Wisdom rejoiceth in a higher aim,
Nor heeds the transient shadows of a day;
These earthly sounds may die away, and all
These perishable pictures sink in night,
But Virtue from the dust her sons shall call,
And lead them forth to joy, and life, and light;
Though from their languid grasp earth's comforts fly,
And with the silent worm their buried bodies lie.

For other scenes there are; and in a clime
Purer, and other strains to earth unknown,
Where heaven's high host, with symphonies sublime,
Sing unto Him that sitteth on the throne.
Enough for man, if he the task fulfil
Which GOD ordained, and to his journey's end
Bear him right on, betide him good or ill;
Then Hope to soothe his death-bed shall descend,
Nor leave him, till in mansions of the blest
He gains his destined home, his everlasting rest.

THE BATTLE OF THE NILE

Shout! for the Lord hath triumphed gloriously!
Upon the shores of that renowned land,
Where erst His mighty arm and outstretched hand
He lifted high,
And dashed, in pieces dashed the enemy;—
Upon that ancient coast,
Where Pharaoh's chariot and his host
He cast into the deep,
Whilst o'er their silent pomp He bid the swoll'n sea sweep;
Upon that eastern shore,
That saw His awful arm revealed of yore,
Again hath He arisen, and opposed
His foes' defying vaunt: o'er them the deep hath closed!

Shades of mighty chiefs of yore,
Who triumphed on the self-same shore:
Ammon, who first o'er ocean's empire wide
Didst bid the bold bark stem the roaring tide;
Sesac, who from the East to farthest West
Didst rear thy pillars over realms subdued;

And thou, whose bones do rest
In the huge pyramid's dim solitude,
Beneath the uncouth stone,
Thy name and deeds unknown;
And Philip's glorious son,
With conquest flushed, for fields and cities won;
And thou, imperial Cæsar, whose sole sway
The long-disputed world at length confessed,
When on these shores thy bleeding rival lay!
Oh, could ye, starting from your long cold rest,
Burst Death's oblivious trance,
And once again with plumed pride advance,
How would ye own your fame surpassed,
And on the sand your trophies cast,
When, the storm of conflict o'er,
And ceased the burning battle's roar,
Beneath the morning's orient light,
Ye saw, with sails all swelling white,
Britain's proud fleet, to many a joyful cry,
Ride o'er the rolling surge in awful sovereignty!

For fierce Ambition fired your mind—
Beside your glittering car,
Amid the thickest war,
Went Superstition, sorceress blind,
In dimly-figured robe, with scowling mien,
Half hid in jealous hood;
And Tyranny, beneath whose helm was seen
His eye suffused with blood;
And giant Pride,
That the great sun with haughty smile defied;
And Avarice, that grasped his guilty gold;
These, as the sorceress her loud sistrum rung,
Their dismal pæan sung;
And still, far off, pale Pity hung her head,
Whilst o'er the dying and the dead
The victor's brazen wheels with gory axle rolled.
Now look on him, in holy courage bold;
The asserter of his country's cause behold!
He lifts his gaze to heaven, serenely brave,
And whilst around war's fearful banners wave,
He prays: Protect us, as our cause is just;
For in thy might alone, Judge of the world, we trust!

And they are scattered—the destroyers die!
They that usurped the bloody victor's claim,
That spoke of freedom; but, behold a cry!
They, that like a wasteful flame,

Or the huge sandy pillar, that amain
Whirls 'mid the silence of the desert plain,
Deathful in their career of terror came,
And scattered ruin as they passed!
So rush they, like the simoom's horrid blast;
They sweep, and all around is wilderness!
But from thy throne on high,
Thou, God, hast heard the cry
Of nations in distress!
Britain goes forth, beneath thy might,
To quell the proud blasphemers in the fight;
And Egypt, far along her winding main,
Echoes the shout of joy, and genuine Freedom's strain!

Now let them, who thy name, O GOD! defy,
Invoke the mighty Prophet of the East;
Or deck, as erst, the mystic feast
To Ashtaroth, queen of the starry sky!
Let them, in some cavern dark,
Seek Osiris' buried ark;
Or call on Typhon, of gigantic form,
Lifting his hundred arms, and howling 'mid the storm!
Or to that grisly king
In vain their cymbals let them ring,
To him in Tophet's vale revered
(With smoke his brazen idol smeared),
Grim Moloch, in whose fuming furnace blue
The unpitying priest the shrieking infant threw,
Whilst to shrill cries, and drums' and timbrels' sound,
The frantic and unhearing troop danced round;
To him despairing let them go,
And tell their fearful tale of hideous overthrow!

Calm breathed the airs along the evening bay,
Where, all in warlike pride,
The Gallic squadron stretched its long array;
And o'er the tranquil tide
With beauteous bend the streamers waved on high
But, ah! how changed the scene ere night descends!
Hark to the shout that heaven's high concave rends!
Hark to that dying cry!
Whilst, louder yet, the cannon's roar
Resounds along the Nile's affrighted shore,
Where, from his oozy bed,
The cowering crocodile hath raised his head!
What bursting flame
Lightens the long track of the gleamy brine!
From yon proud ship it came,

That towered the leader of the hostile line!
Now loud explosion rends the midnight air!
Heard ye the last deep groaning of despair?
Heaven's fiery cope unwonted thunders fill,
Then, with one dreadful pause, earth, air, and seas are still!

But now the mingled fight
Begins its awful strife again!
Through the dun shades of night
Along the darkly-heaving main
Is seen the frequent flash;
And many a towering mast with dreadful crash
Rings falling. Is the scene of slaughter o'er?
Is the death-cry heard no more?
Lo! where the East a glimmering freckle streaks,
Slow o'er the shadowy wave the gray dawn breaks.
Behold, O Sun, the flood
Strewed with the dead, and dark with blood!
Behold, all scattered on the rocking tide,
The wrecks of haughty Gallia's pride!
But Britain's floating bulwarks, with serene
And silent pomp, amid the deathful scene
Move glorious, and more beautiful display
Their ensigns streaming to thy orient ray.

Awful Genius of the land!
Who (thy reign of glory closed)
By marble wrecks, half-hid in sand,
Hast mournfully reposed;
Who long, amid the wasteful desert wide,
Hast loved with death-like stillness to abide;
Or wrapped in tenfold gloom,
From noise of human things for ages hid,
Hast sat upon the shapeless tomb
In the forlorn and dripping pyramid;
Awake! Arise!
Though thou behold the day no more
That saw thy pride and pomp of yore;
Though, like the sounds that in the morning ray
Trembled and died away
From Memnon's statue; though, like these, the voice
That bade thy vernal plains rejoice,
The voice of Science, is no longer heard;
And all thy gorgeous state hath disappeared:
Yet hear, with triumph, and with hope again,
The shouts of joy that swell from thy forsaken main!

And, oh! might He, at whose command

Deep darkness shades a mourning land;
At whose command, bursting from night,
And flaming with redoubled light,
The Sun of Science mounts again,
And re-illumes the wide-extended plain!
Might He, from this eventful day,
Illustrious Egypt, to thy shore
Science, Freedom, Peace restore,
And bid thy crowded ports their ancient pomp display!
No more should Superstition mark,
In characters uncouth and dark,
Her dreary, monumental shrine!
No more should meek-eyed Piety
Outcast, insulted lie
Beneath the mosque, whose golden crescents shine,
But starting from her trance,
O'er Nubia's sands advance
Beyond the farthest fountains of the Nile!
The dismal Gallas should behold her smile,
And Abyssinia's inmost rocks rejoice
To hear her awful lore, yet soft consoling voice!

Hasten, O GOD! the time, when never more
Pale Pity, from her moonlight seat shall hear,
And dropping at the sound a fruitless tear,
The far-off battle's melancholy roar;
When never more Horror's portentous cry
Shall sound amid the troubled sky;
Or dark Destruction's grimly-smiling mien,
Through the red flashes of the fight be seen!
Father in heaven! our ardent hopes fulfil;
Thou speakest "Peace," and the vexed world is still!
Yet should Oppression huge arise,
And with bloody banners spread,
Upon the gasping nations tread,
Whilst he thy name defies,
Trusting in Thee alone, we hope to quell
His furious might, his purpose fell;
And as the ensigns of his baffled pride
O'er the seas are scattered wide,
We will take up a joyous strain and cry—
Shout! for the Lord hath triumphed gloriously!

A GARDEN-SEAT AT HOME

Oh, no; I would not leave thee, my sweet home,

Decked with the mantling woodbine and the rose,
And slender woods that the still scene inclose,
For yon magnificent and ample dome
That glitters in my sight! yet I can praise
Thee, Arundel, who, shunning the thronged ways
Of glittering vice, silently dost dispense
The blessings of retired munificence.
Me, a sequestered cottage, on the verge
Of thy outstretched domain, delights; and here
I wind my walks, and sometimes drop a tear
O'er Harriet's urn, scarce wishing to emerge
Into the troubled ocean of that life,
Where all is turbulence, and toil, and strife.
Calm roll the seasons o'er my shaded niche;
I dip the brush, or touch the tuneful string,
Or hear at eve the unscared blackbirds sing;
Enough if, from their loftier sphere, the rich
Deign my abode to visit, and the poor
Depart not, cold and hungry, from my door.

IN HORTO REV. J. STILL, APUD KNOYLE, VILLAM AMOENISSIMAM

Stranger! a while beneath this aged tree
Rest thee, the hills beyond, and flowery meads,
Surveying; and if Nature's charms may wake
A sweet and silent transport at thine heart,
In spring-time, whilst the bee hums heedless nigh,
Rejoice! for thee the verdant spot is dressed,
Circled with laurels green, and sprinkled o'er
With many a budding rose: the shrubs all ring
To the birds' warblings, and by fits the air
Whispers amid the foliage o'er thine head!
Rejoice, and oh! if life's sweet spring be thine,
So gather its brief rose-buds, and deceive
The cares and crosses of humanity.

GREENWICH HOSPITAL

Come to these peaceful seats, and think no more
Of cold, of midnight watchings, or the roar
Of Ocean, tossing on his restless bed!
Come to these peaceful seats, ye who have bled
For honour, who have traversed the great flood,
Or on the battle's front with stern eye stood,

When rolled its thunder, and the billows red
Oft closed, with sudden flashings, o'er the dead!
Oh, heavy are the sorrows that beset
Old age! and hard it is—hard to forget
The sunshine of our youth, our manhood's pride!
But here, O aged men! ye may abide
Secure, and see the last light on the wave
Of Time, which wafts you silent to your grave;
Like the calm evening ray, that smiles serene
Upon the tranquil Thames, and cheers the sinking scene.

A RUSTIC SEAT NEAR THE SEA

To him, who, many a night upon the main,
At mid-watch, from the bounding vessel's side,
Shivering, has listened to the rocking tide,
Oh, how delightful smile thy views again,
Fair Land! the sheltered hut, and far-seen mill
That safe sails round and round; the tripping rill
That o'er the gray sand glitters; the clear sky,
Beneath whose blue vault shines the village tower,
That high elms, swaying in the wind, embower;
And hedge-rows, where the small birds' melody
Solace the lithe and loitering peasant lad!
O Stranger! is thy pausing fancy sad
At thought of many evils which do press
On wide humanity!—Look up; address
The GOD who made the world; but let thy heart
Be thankful, though some heavy thoughts have part,
That, sheltered from the human storms' career,
Thou meetest innocence and quiet here.

WARDOUR CASTLE

If rich designs of sumptuous art may please,
Or Nature's loftier views, august and old,
Stranger! behold this spreading scene;—behold
This amphitheatre of aged trees,
That solemn wave above thee, and around
Darken the towering hills! Dost thou complain
That thou shouldst cope with penury or pain,
Or sigh to think what pleasures might be found
Amid such wide possessions!—Pause awhile;
Imagine thou dost see the sick man smile;

See the pale exiles, that in yonder dome,
Safe from the wasteful storm, have found a home;
And thank the Giver of all good, that lent
To the humane, retired, beneficent,
The power to bless. Nor lift thy heart elate,
If such domains be thine; but emulate
The fair example, and those deeds, that rise
Like holy incense wafted to the skies;
Those deeds that shall sustain the conscious soul,
When all this empty world hath perished, like a scroll!

POLE-VELLUM, CORNWALL

A PICTURESQUE COTTAGE AND GROUNDS BELONGING TO J. LEMON, ESQ.

Stranger! mark this lovely scene,
When the evening sets serene,
And starting o'er the silent wood,
The last pale sunshine streaks the flood,
And the water gushing near
Soothes, with ceaseless drip, thine ear;
Then bid each passion sink to rest;—
Should ev'n one wish rise in thy breast,
One tender wish, as now in mine,
That some such quiet spot were thine,
And thou, recalling seasons fled,
Couldst wake the slumbers of the dead,
And bring back her you loved, to share
With thee calm peace and comfort there;—
Oh, check the thought, but inly pray
To HE, "who gives and takes away,"
That many years this fair domain
Its varied beauties may retain;—
So when some wanderer, who has lost
His heart's best treasure, who has crossed
In life bleak hills and passes rude,
Should gain this lovely solitude;
Delighted he may pause a while,
And when he marks the landscape smile,
Leave with its willows, ere he part,
The blessings of a softened heart.

ON A BEAUTIFUL SPRING, FORMING A COLD BATH, AT COOMBE, NEAR DONHEAD, BELONGING TO MY BROTHER, CHAS. BOWLES, ESQ.

Fountain, that sparklest through the shady place,
Making a soft, sad murmur o'er the stones
That strew thy lucid way! Oh, if some guest
Should haply wander near, with slow disease
Smitten, may thy cold springs the rose of health
Bring back, and the quick lustre to his eye!
The ancient oaks that on thy margin wave,
The song of birds, and through the rocky cave
The clear stream gushing, their according sounds
Should mingle, and, like some strange music, steal
Sadly, yet soothing, o'er his aching breast.
And thou, pale exile from thy native shores,
Here drink,—oh, couldst thou!—as of Lethe's stream!
Nor friends, nor bleeding country, nor the views
Of hills or streams beloved, nor vesper bell,
Heard in the twilight vale, remember more!

A CENOTAPH, TO THE MEMORY OF LIEUTENANT-COLONEL ISAAC, WHO DIED AT CAPE ST NICHOLA MOLE.

Oh, hadst thou fall'n, brave youth! on that proud day,
When our victorious fleet o'er the red surge
Rolled in terrific glory, thou hadst fall'n
Most honoured; and Remembrance, while she thought
Upon thy gallant end, had dried her tear!
Now far beyond the huge Atlantic wave
Thy bones decay; the withering pestilence,
That swept the islands of the western world,
Smote thee, untimely drooping to the tomb!
But 'tis enough; whate'er a soldier's fate,
That firm he hied him, where stern honour bade;
Though with unequal strength, he sunk and died.

The st of June , when Colonel Isaac greatly distinguished
himself as commander of the military on board Lord Howe's ship.

TRANSLATION OF A LATIN POEM BY THE REV. NEWTON OGLE, DEAN OF MANCHESTER

Oh thou, that prattling on thy pebbled way
Through my paternal vale dost stray,
Working thy shallow passage to the sea!
Oh, stream, thou speedest on
The same as many seasons gone;

But not, alas, to me
Remain the feelings that beguiled
My early road, when, careless and content,
(Losing the hours in pastimes innocent)
Upon thy banks I strayed a playful child;
Whether the pebbles that thy margin strew,
Collecting, heedlessly I threw;
Or loved in thy translucent wave
My tender shrinking feet to lave;
Or else ensnared your little fry,
And thought how wondrous skilled was I!
So passed my boyish days, unknown to pain,
Days that will ne'er return again.
It seems but yesterday
I was a child, to-morrow to be gray!
So years succeeding years steal silently away.
Not fleeter thy own current, hurrying thee,
Rolls down to the great sea.
Thither oh carry these sad thoughts; the deep
Bury them!—thou, meantime, thy tenor keep,
And winding through the green-wood, cheer,
As erst, my native, peaceful pastures here.

ST MICHAEL'S MOUNT. INSCRIBED TO THE RIGHT HONOURABLE LORD SOMERS

While summer airs scarce breathe along the tide,
Oft pausing, up the mountain's craggy side
We climb, how beautiful, how still, how clear,
The scenes that stretch around! The rocks that rear
Their shapes, in rich fantastic colours dressed;
The hill-tops, where the softest shadows rest;
The long-retiring bay, the level sand,
The fading sea-line, and the furthest land,
That seems, as low it lessens from the eye,
To steal away beneath the cloudless sky!
But yesterday, the misty morn was spread
In dreariness on the bleak mountain's head;
No glittering prospect from the upland smiled,
The driving squall came dark, the sea heaved wild,
And, lost and lonely, the wayfarer sighed,
Wet with the hoar spray of the flashing tide.
How changed is now the circling scene! The deep
Stirs not; the glancing roofs and white towers peep
Along the margin of the lucid bay;
The sails, descried far in the offing gray,
Hang motionless, and the pale headland's height

Is touched as with sweet gleams of fairy light!
Oh, lives there on earth's busy-stirring scene,
Whom Nature's tranquil charms, her airs serene,
Her seas, her skies, her sunbeams, fail to move
With stealing tenderness and grateful love!
Go, thankless man, to Misery's cave—behold
Captivity, stretched in her dungeon cold!
Or think on those who, in yon dreary mine,
Sunk fathoms deep beneath the rolling brine,
From year to year, amid the lurid shade,
O'er-wearied, ply their melancholy trade;
That thou may'st bless the glorious sun; and hail
Him who with beauty clothed the hill and vale;
Who bent the arch of the high heavens for thee,
And stretched in amplitude the broad blue sea!
Now sunk are all its murmurs; and the air
But moves by fits the bents, that here and there
Upshoot in casual spots of faded green:
Here straggling sheep the scanty pasture glean,
Or, on the jutting fragments that impend,
Stray fearlessly, and gaze, as we ascend.
Mountain, no pomp of waving woods hast thou,
That deck with varied shade thy hoary brow;
No sunny meadows at thy feet are spread,
No streamlets sparkle o'er their pebbly bed!
But thou canst boast thy beauties: ample views
That catch the rapt eye of the pausing Muse;
Headlands around new-lighted; sails, and seas,
Now glassy-smooth, now wrinkling to the breeze;
And when the drisly Winter, wrapped in sleet,
Goes by, and winds and rain thy ramparts beat,
Fancy can see thee standing thus aloof,
And frowning, bleak, and bare, and tempest-proof,
Look as with awful confidence, and brave
The howling hurricane, the dashing wave;
More graceful, when the storm's dark vapours frown,
Than when the summer suns in pomp go down!
And such is he, who, clad in watchet weeds,
And boasting little more than nature needs,
Can wrap him in contentedness, and wear
A port unchanged, in seasons rude or fair.
His may be Fancy's sunshine, and the Muse
May deck his visions with her fairest hues;
And he may lift his honest front, and say
To the hard storm, that rends his locks of gray,
I heed thee not;—he unappalled may stand
Beneath the cloud that shades a sinking land,
While heedless of the storm that onward sweeps,

Mad, impious Riot his loud wassail keeps,
Pre-eminent in native worth; nor bend,
Though gathering ills on his bare head descend:
And when the wasteful storm sweeps o'er its prey,
And rends the kingdoms of the world away,
He, firm as stands the rock's unshaken base,
Yet panting for a surer resting-place,
The human hurricane unmoved can see,
And say, O GOD, my refuge is in Thee!
States, anchored deep, that far their shadow cast,
Rock, and are scattered by the ALMIGHTY'S blast;
As when, awakened from his horrid sleep,
In fiery caves, a thousand fathoms deep,
The Earthquake's Demon hies aloft; he waits,
Nigh some high-turreted proud city's gates,
As listening to the mingled shouts and din
Of the mad crowd that feast or dance within.
Mean time sad Nature feels his sway, the wave
Heaves, and low sounds moan through the mountain cave;
Then all at once is still, still as midnight,
When not the lime-leaf moves: Oh, piteous sight!
For now the glittering domes crash from on high—
And hark, a strange and lamentable cry!
It ceases, and the tide's departing roar
Alone is heard upon the desert shore,
That, as it sweeps with slow huge swell away,
Remorseless mutters o'er its buried prey.
So Ruin hurrieth o'er this shaken ball:
He bids his blast go forth, and lo! doth fall
A Carthage or a Rome. Then rolls the tide
Of deep Forgetfulness, whelming the pride
Of man, his shattered and forsaken bowers,
His noiseless cities, and his prostrate towers.
Some columns, eminent and awful, stand,
Like Egypt's pillars on the lonely sand;
We read upon their base, inscribed by Fame,
A HOMER'S here, or here a SHAKESPEARE'S name;
Yet think not of the surge, that soon may sweep
Ourselves unnumbered to the oblivious deep.
Yet time has been, as mouldering legends say,
When all yon western tract, and this bright bay,
Where now the sunshine sleeps, and wheeling white
The sea-mew circles in fantastic flight,
Was peopled wide; but the loud storm hath raved,
Where its green top the high wood whispering waved,
And many a year the slowly-rising flood
Raked, where the Druids' uncouth altar stood.
Thou only, aged mountain, dost remain,

Stern monument amidst the deluged plain!
And fruitless the big waves thy bulwarks beat;
The big waves slow retire, and murmur at thy feet:
Thou, half-encircled by the refluent tide,
As if thy state its utmost rage defied,
Dost tower above the scene, as in thine ancient pride.
Mountain! the curious Muse might love to gaze
On the dim record of thy early days;
Oft fancying that she heard, like the low blast,
The sounds of mighty generations past.
Thee the Phoenician, as remote he sailed
Along the unknown coast, exulting hailed,
And when he saw thy rocky point aspire,
Thought on his native shores of Aradus or Tyre.
Distained with many a ghastly giant's blood,
Upon thy height huge Corineus stood,
And clashed his shield; whilst, hid in caves profound,
His monstrous foe cowered at the fearful sound.
Hark to the brazen clarion's pealing swell!
The shout at intervals, the deepening yell!
Long ages speed away, yet now again
The noise of battle hurtles on the plain!
Behold the dark-haired warriors!—down thy side,
O mountain! sternly terrible, they stride!
Ev'n now, impatient for the promised war,
They rear their axes huge, and shouting, cry to Thor.
The sounds of conflict cease—at dead of night
A voice is heard: Prepare the Druid rite!
And hark! the bard upon thy summit rings
The deep chords of his thrilling harp, and sings
To Night's pale Queen, that through the heavens wide,
Amidst her still host list'ning seems to ride!
Slow sinks the cadence of the solemn lay,
And all the sombrous scenery steals away—
The shadowy Druid throng, the darksome wood,
And the hoar altar, wet with human blood!
Marked ye the Angel-spectre that appeared?
By other hands the holy fane is reared
High on the point, where, gazing o'er the flood,
Confessed, the glittering apparition stood.
And now the sailor, on his watch of night,
Sees, like a glimmering star, the far-off light;
Or, homeward bound, hears on the twilight bay
The slowly-chanted vespers die away!
These scenes are fled and passed, yet still sublime,
And wearing graceful the gray tints of Time,
Upon the steep rock's craggy eminence
The embattled castle sits, surveying thence

The villages that strew the subject plain,
And the long winding of the lucid main:
Meantime the stranger marks its turrets high,
And muses on the tale of changeful years gone by.
Of this no more: lo! here our journey ends;
Wide and more wide the arch of heaven extends,
And on this topmost fragment as we lean,
We feel removed from dim earth's distant scene.
Lift up the hollow trump that on the ground
Is cast, and let it, rolling its long sound,
Speak to the surge below, that we may gain
Tidings from those who traverse the wide main.
Or tread we now some spot of wizard-land,
And mark the sable trump, that may command
The brazen doors to fly, and with loud call
Scare the grim giant in his murky hall!
Hail, solitary castle! that dost crown
This desert summit, and supreme look down
On the long-lessening landscape stretched below;
Fearless to trace thy inmost haunts we go!
We climb the steps:—No warning signs are sent,
No fiery shapes flash on the battlement.
We enter; the long chambers without fear
We traverse; no strange echoes meet the ear;
No time-worn tapestry spontaneous shakes,
No spell-bound maiden from her trance awakes,
But Taste's fair hand arrays the peaceful dome,
And hither the domestic virtues come;
Pleased, while to this secluded scene they bear
Sweets that oft wither in a world of care.
Castle! no more thou frownest on the main
In the dark terror of thy ancient reign;
No more thy long and dreary halls affright,
Swept by the stoled spirits of the night;
But calm, and heedless of the storms that beat,
Here Elegance and Peace assume their seat;
And when the night descends, and Ocean roars,
Rocking without upon his darkened shores,
These vaulted roofs to gentle sounds reply,
The voice of social cheer, or song of harmony.
So fade the modes of life with slow decay,
And various ages various hues display!
Fled are the grimly shadows of Romance—
And, pleased, we see in beauteous troop advance
New arts, new manners, from the Gothic gloom
Escaped, and scattering flowers that sweetlier bloom!
Refinement wakes; before her beaming eye
Dispersed, the fumes of feudal darkness fly.

Like orient Morning on the mountain's head,
A softer light on life's wide scene is shed;
Lapping in bliss the sense of human cares,
Hark! Melody pours forth her sweetest airs;
And like the shades that on the still lake lie,
Of rocks, or fringing woods, or tinted sky,
Painting her hues on the clear tablet lays,
And her own beauteous world with tender touch displays!
Then Science lifts her form, august and fair,
And shakes the night-dews from her glittering hair;
Meantime rich Culture clothes the living waste,
And purer patterns of Athenian Taste
Invite the eye, and wake the kindling sense;
And milder Manners, as they play, dispense,
Like tepid airs of Spring, their genial influence!
Such is thy boast, Refinement. But deep dyes
Oft mar the splendour of thy noontide skies:
Then Fancy, sick of follies that deform
The face of day, and in the sunshine swarm;
Sick of the fluttering fopperies that engage
The vain pursuits of a degenerate age;
Sick of smooth Sophistry's insidious cant,
Or cold Impiety's defying rant;
Sick of the muling sentiment that sighs
O'er its dead bird, while Want unpitied cries;
Sick of the pictures that pale Lust inflame,
And flush the cheek of Love with deep, deep shame;
Would fain the shade of elder days recall,
The Gothic battlements, the bannered hall;
Or list of elfin harps the fabling rhyme,
Or wrapped in melancholy trance sublime,
Pause o'er the working of some wond'rous tale,
Or bid the spectres of the castle hail!
Oh, might I now, amid the frowning storm,
Behold, great Vision of the Mount! thy form,
Such and so vast as thou wert seen of yore,
When looking steadfast to Bayonna's shore,
Thou sattest awful on the topmost stone,
Making the rock thy solitary throne!
For up the narrow steps, winding with pain,
The watch-tower's loftiest platform now we gain.
Departed spirit! fruitless is the prayer,
We see alone thy long-deserted chair;
And never more, or in the storm of night,
Or by the glimmering moon's illusive light,
Or when the flash, with red and hasty glance,
Sudden illumes the sea's remote expanse,
The shores, the cliffs, the mountain, till again

Deep darkness closes on the roaring main,
Shalt thou, dread Angel, with unaltered mien,
Sublime upon thy cloudy seat be seen!
Yet, musing much on wild tradition's lore,
And many a phantom tale, believed of yore,
Chiefly remembering the sweet song (whose strain
Shall never die) of him who wept in vain
For his loved Lycidas, in the wide sea
Whelmed, when he cried, great Angel, unto thee,
The fabled scene of thy renown we trace,
And hail, with thronging thoughts, thy hallowed resting-place!
The stealing Morn goes out—here let us end
Fitliest our song, and to the shore descend.
Yet once more, azure ocean, and once more,
Ye lighted headlands, and thou stretching shore,
Down on the beauties of your scenes we cast
A tender look, the longest and the last!
Amid the arch of heaven, extended clear,
Scarce the thin flecks of feathery clouds appear;
Beyond the long curve of the lessening bay
The still Atlantic stretches its bright way;
The tall ship moves not on the tranquil brine;
Around, the solemn promontories shine;
No sounds approach us, save, at times, the cry
Of the gray gull, that scarce is heard so high;
The billows make no noise, and on the breast
Of charmed Ocean, Silence sinks to rest!
Oh, might we thus from heaven's bright battlements
Behold the scene Humanity presents;
And see, like this, all harmonised and still,
And hear no far-off sounds of earthly ill!
Wide landscape of the world, in purest light
Arrayed, how fair, how cheering were the sight!
Alas! we think upon this seat of care,
And ask, if peace, if harmony be there.
We hear the clangours and the cries that shake
The mad world, and their dismal music make;
We see gaunt Vice, of dread, enormous size,
That fearless in the broad day sweltering lies,
And scorns the feeble arrow that assails
His Heaven-defying crest and iron scales;
His brows with wan and withered roses crowned,
And reeling to the pipe's lascivious sound,
We see Intemperance his goblet quaff;
And mocking Blasphemy, with mad loud laugh,
Acting before high Heaven a direr part,
Sport with the weapons that shall pierce his heart!
If o'er the southern wave we turn our sight,

More dismal shapes of hideous woe affright:
Grim-visaged War, that ruthless, as he hies,
Drowns with his trumpet's blast a brother's cries;
And Massacre, by yelling furies led,
With ghastly grin and eye-balls rolling red!
O'er a vast field, wide heaped with festering slain,
Hark! how the Demon Passions shout amain,
And cry, exulting, while the death-storm lowers,
Hurrah! the kingdoms of the world are ours!
O GOD! who madest man, I see these things,
And wearied wish for a fleet angel's wings,
That I might fly away, and hear no more
The surge that moans along this mortal shore!
But Joy's unclouded sunshine may not be,
Till, Father of all worlds, we rest with Thee!
Then Truth, uplifting from thy works the pall,
Shall speak: In wisdom hast Thou made them all;
Then angels and archangels, as they gaze,
And all the acclaiming host of heaven, shall raise
The loud hosannah of eternal praise!
Here all is mixed with sorrow; and the clouds
Hang awfully, whose shade the dim earth shrouds;
Therefore I mourn for man, and sighing say,
As down the steep I wind my homeward way,
Oh, when will Earth's long muttering tempests cease,
And all be sunshine (like this scene) and peace!

ON AN UNFORTUNATE AND BEAUTIFUL WOMAN

Oh, Mary, when distress and anguish came,
And slow disease preyed on thy wasted frame;
When every friend, ev'n like thy bloom, was fled,
And Want bowed low thy unsupported head;
Sure sad Humanity a tear might give,
And Virtue say, Live, beauteous sufferer, live!
But should there one be found, (amidst the few
Who with compassion thy last pangs might view),
One who beheld thy errors with a tear,
To whom the ruins of thy heart were dear,
Who fondly hoped, the ruthful season past,
Thy faded virtues might revive at last;
Should such be found—oh! when he saw thee lie,
Closing on every earthly hope thine eye;
When he beheld despair, with rueful trace,
Mark the strange features of thy altered face;
When he beheld, as painful death drew nigh,

Thy pale, pale cheek, thy feebly lifted eye,
Thy chill, shrunk hand, hung down as in despair,
Or slowly raised, with many a muttered prayer;—
When thus, in early youth, he saw thee bend
Poor to the grave, and die without a friend;
Some sadder feelings might unbidden start,
And more than common pity touch his heart!
The eventful scene is closed; with pausing dread
And sorrow I drew nigh the silent bed;
Thy look was calm—thy heart was cold and still,
As if the world had never used it ill;
Methought the last faint smile, with traces weak,
Still seemed to linger on thy faded cheek.
Poor Mary! though most beauteous in thy face,
Ere sorrow touched it, beamed each lovely grace;
Yet, oh! thy living features never wore
A look so sweet, so eloquent before,
As this, which bids all human passions cease,
And tells my pitying heart you died in peace!

HYMN TO WODEN

God of the battle, hear our prayer!
By the lifted falchion's glare;
By the uncouth fane sublime,
Marked with many a Runic rhyme;
By the "weird sisters" dread,
That, posting through the battle red,
Choose the slain, and with them go
To Valhalla's halls below,
Where the phantom-chiefs prolong
Their echoing feast, a giant throng,
And their dreadful beverage drain
From the skulls of warriors slain:
God of the battle, hear our prayer;
And may we thy banquet share!
Save us, god, from slow disease;
From pains that the brave spirit freeze;
From the burning fever's rage;
From wailings of unhonoured age,
Drawing painful his last breath;
Give us in the battle death!
Let us lift our glittering shield,
And perish, perish in the field!
Now o'er Cumri's hills of snow
To death, or victory, we go;

Hark! the chiefs their cars prepare;
See! they bind their yellow hair;
Frenzy flashes from their eye,
They fly—our foes before them fly!
Woden, in thy empire drear,
Thou the groans of death dost hear,
And welcome to thy dusky hall
Those that for their country fall!
Hail, all hail the godlike train,
That with thee the goblet drain;
Or with many a huge compeer,
Lift, as erst, the shadowy spear!
Whilst Hela's inmost caverns dread
Echo to their giant tread,
And ten thousand thousand shields
Flash lightning o'er the glimmering fields!
Hark! the battle-shouts begin—
Louder sounds the glorious din:
Louder than the ice's roar,
Bursting on the thawing shore;
Or crashing pines that strew the plain,
When the whirlwinds hurl the main!
Riding through the death-field red,
And singling fast the destined dead,
See the fatal sisters fly!
Now my throbbing breast beats high—
Now I urge my panting steed,
Where the foemen thickest bleed.
Soon exulting I shall go,
Woden, to thy halls below;
Or o'er the victims, as they die,
Chaunt the song of Victory!

COOMBE-ELLEN

Call the strange spirit that abides unseen
In wilds, and wastes, and shaggy solitudes,
And bid his dim hand lead thee through these scenes
That burst immense around! By mountains, glens,
And solitary cataracts that dash
Through dark ravines; and trees, whose wreathed roots
O'erhang the torrent's channelled course; and streams,
That far below, along the narrow vale,
Upon their rocky way wind musical.
Stranger! if Nature charm thee, if thou lovest
To trace her awful steps, in glade or glen,

Or under covert of the rocking wood,
That sways its murmuring and mossy boughs
Above thy head; now, when the wind at times
Stirs its deep silence round thee, and the shower
Falls on the sighing foliage, hail her here
In these her haunts; and, rapt in musings high,
Think that thou holdest converse with some Power
Invisible and strange; such as of yore
Greece, in the shades of piney Mænalaus,
The abode of Pan, or Ida's hoary caves,
Worshipped; and our old Druids, 'mid the gloom
Of rocks and woods like these, with muttered spell
Invoked, and the loud ring of choral harps.
Hast thou oft mourned the chidings of the world,
The sound of her disquiet, that ascends
For ever, mocking the high throne of GOD!
Hast thou in youth known sorrow! Hast thou drooped,
Heart-stricken, over youth's and beauty's grave,
And ever after thought on the sad sound
The cold earth made, which, cast into the vault,
Consigned thy heart's best treasure—dust to dust!
Here, lapped into a sweet forgetfulness,
Hang o'er the wreathed waterfall, and think
Thou art alone in this dark world and wide!
Here Melancholy, on the pale crags laid,
Might muse herself to sleep; or Fancy come,
Witching the mind with tender cozenage,
And shaping things that are not; here all day
Might Meditation listen to the lapse
Of the white waters, flashing through the cleft,
And, gazing on the many shadowing trees,
Mingle a pensive moral as she gazed.
High o'er thy head, amidst the shivered slate,
Behold, a sapling yet, the wild ash bend,
Its dark red berries clustering, as it wished
In the clear liquid mirror, ere it fell,
To trace its beauties; o'er the prone cascade,
Airy, and light, and elegant, the birch
Displays its glossy stem, amidst the gloom
Of alders and jagged fern, and evermore
Waves her light pensile foliage, as she wooed
The passing gale to whisper flatteries.
Upon the adverse bank, withered, and stripped
Of all its pleasant leaves, a scathed oak
Hangs desolate, once sovereign of the scene,
Perhaps, proud of its beauty and its strength,
And branching its broad arms along the glen:
Oh, speaks it no remonstrance to the heart!

It seems to say: So shall the spoiler come,
The season that shall shatter your fair leaves,
Gay children of the summer! yet enjoy
Your pleasant prime, and lift your green heads high,
Exulting; but the storm will come at last,
That shall lay low your strength, and give your pride
To the swift-hurrying stream of age, like mine.
And so severe Experience oft reproves
The gay and careless children of the world;
They hear the cold rebuke, and then again
Turn to their sport, as likes them, and dance on!
And let them dance; so all their blooming prime
They give not up to vanity, but learn
That wisdom and that virtue which shall best
Avail them, when the evil days draw nigh,
And the brief blossoms of their spring-time fade.
Now wind we up the glen, and hear below
The dashing torrent, in deep woods concealed,
And now again white-flashing on the view,
O'er the huge craggy fragments. Ancient stream,
That murmurest through the mountain solitudes,
The time has been when no eye marked thy course,
Save His who made the world! Fancy might dream
She saw thee thus bound on from age to age
Unseen of man, whilst awful Nature sat
On the rent rocks, and said: These haunts be mine.
Now Taste has marked thy features; here and there
Touching with tender hand, but injuring not,
Thy beauties; whilst along thy woody verge
Ascends the winding pathway, and the eye
Catches at intervals thy varied falls.
But loftier scenes invite us; pass the hill,
And through the woody hanging, at whose feet
The tinkling Ellen winds, pursue thy way.
Yon bleak and weather-whitened rock, immense,
Upshoots amidst the scene, craggy and steep,
And like some high-embattled citadel,
That awes the low plain shadowing. Half-way up
The purple heath is seen, but bare its brow,
And deep-intrenched, and all beneath it spread
With massy fragments riven from its top.
Amidst the crags, and scarce discerned so high,
Hangs here and there a sheep, by its faint bleat
Discovered, whilst the astonished eye looks up,
And marks it on the precipice's brink
Pick its scant food secure:—and fares it not
Ev'n so with you, poor orphans, ye who climb
The rugged path of life without a friend;

And over broken crags bear hardly on,
With pale imploring looks, that seem to say,
My mother! she is buried, and at rest,
Laid in her grave-clothes; and the heart is still,
The only heart that throughout all the world
Beat anxiously for you! Oh, yet bear on;
He who sustains the bleating lamb shall feed
And comfort you: meantime the heaven's pure beam,
That breaks above the sable mountain's brow,
Lighting, one after one, the sunless crags,
Awakes the blissful confidence, that here,
Or in a world where sorrow never comes,
All shall be well.
Now through the whispering wood
We steal, and mark the old and mossy oaks
Imboss the mountain slope; or the wild ash,
With rich red clusters mantling; or the birch,
In lonely glens light-wavering; till behold!
The rapid river shooting through the gloom
Its lucid line along; and on its side
The bordering pastures green, where the swinked ox
Lies dreaming, heedless of the numerous flies
That, in the transitory sunshine, hum
Round his broad breast; and further up the cot,
With blue, light smoke ascending; images
Of peace and comfort! The wild rocks around
Endear your smile the more, and the full mind,
Sliding from scenes of dread magnificence,
Sinks on your charms reposing; such repose
The sage may feel, when, filled and half-oppressed
With vast conceptions, smiling he returns
To life's consoling sympathies, and hears,
With heartfelt tenderness, the bells ring out;
Or pipe upon the mountains; or the low
Of herds slow winding down the cottaged vale,
Where day's last sunshine linger. Such repose
He feels, who, following where his SHAKSPEARE leads,
As in a dream, through an enchanted land,
Here, with Macbeth, in the dread cavern hails
The weird sisters, and the dismal deed
Without a name; there sees the charmed isle,
The lone domain of Prospero; and, hark!
Wild music, such as earth scarce seems to own,
And Ariel o'er the slow-subsiding surge
Singing her smooth air quaintly! Such repose
Steals o'er her spirits, when, through storms at sea,
Fancy has followed some nigh-foundered bark
Full many a league, in ocean's solitude

Tossed far beyond the Cape of utmost Horn,
That stems the roaring deep; her dreary track
Still Fancy follows, and at dead of night
Hears, with strange thunder, the huge fragments fall
Crashing, from mountains of high-drifting ice
That o'er her bows gleam fearful; till at last
She hails the gallant ship in some still bay
Safe moored; or of delightful Tinian;
Smiling, like fairy isle, amid the waste;
Or of New Zealand, where from sheltering rocks
The clear cascades gush beautiful, and high
The woodland scenery towers above the mast,
Whose long and wavy ensign streams beneath.
Far inland, clad in snow, the mountains lift
Their spiry summits, and endear the more
The sylvan scene around; the healing air
Breathes o'er green myrtles, and the poe-bird flits,
Amid the shade of aromatic shrubs,
With silver neck and blue enamelled wing.
Now cross the stream, and up the narrow track,
That winds along the mountain's edge, behold
The peasant girl ascend: cheerful her look,
Beneath the umbrage of her broad black hat,
And loose her dark-brown hair; the plodding pad
That bears her panting climbs, and with sure step
Avoids the jutting fragments; she, meantime,
Sits unconcerned, till, lessening from the view,
She gains the summit and is seen no more.
All day, along that mountain's heathy waste,
Booted and strapped, and in rough coat succinct,
His small shrill whistle pendent at his breast,
With dogs and gun, untired the sportsman roams;
Nor quits his wildly-devious range, till eve,
Upon the woods, the rocks, and mazy rills
Descending, warns him home: then he rejoins
The social circle, just as the clear moon,
Emerging o'er the sable mountain, sails
Silent, and calm, and beautiful, and sheds
Its solemn grandeur on the shadowy scene.
To music then; and let some chosen strain
Of HANDEL gently recreate the sense,
And give the silent heart to tender joy.
Pass on to the hoar cataract, that foams
Through the dark fissures of the riven rock;
Prone-rushing it descends, and with white whirl,
Save where some silent shady pool receives
Its dash; thence bursting, with collected sweep,
And hollow sound, it hurries, till it falls

Foaming in the wild stream that winds below.
Dark trees, that to the mountain's height ascend,
O'ershade with pendent boughs its mossy course,
And, looking up, the eye beholds it flash
Beneath the incumbent gloom, from ledge to ledge
Shooting its silvery foam, and far within
Wreathing its curve fantastic. If the harp
Of deep poetic inspiration, struck
At times by the pale minstrel, whilst a strange
And beauteous light filled his uplifted eye,
Hath ever sounded into mortal ears,
Here I might think I heard its tones, and saw,
Sublime amidst the solitary scene,
With dimly-gleaming harp, and snowy stole,
And cheek in momentary frenzy flushed,
The great musician stand. Hush, every wind
That shakes the murmuring branches! and thou stream,
Descending still with hollow-sounding sweep,
Hush! 'Twas the bard struck the loud strings: Arise,
Son of the magic song, arise!
And bid the deep-toned lyre
Pour forth its manly melodies.
With eyes on fire,
CARADOC rushed upon the foe;
He reared his arm—he laid the mighty low!
O'er the plain see him urge his gore-bathed steed!
They bleed, the Romans bleed!
He lifts his lance on high,
They fly! the fierce invaders fly!
Fear not now the horse or spear,
Fear not now the foeman's might;
Victory the cry shall hear
Of those who for their country fight;
O'er the slain
That strew the plain,
Stern on her sable war-horse shall she ride,
And lift her red right hand, in their heart's blood deep dyed!
Return, my Muse! the fearful sound is past;
And now a little onward, where the way
Ascends above the oaks that far below
Shade the rude steep, let Contemplation lead
Our footsteps; from this shady eminence
'Tis pleasant and yet fearful to look down
Upon the river roaring, and far off
To see it stretch in peace, and mark the rocks
One after one, in solemn majesty
Unfolding their wild reaches; here with wood
Mantled, beyond abrupt and bare, and each

As if it strove, with emulous disdain,
To tower in ruder, darker amplitude.
Pause, ere we enter the long craggy vale;
It seems the abode of Solitude. So high
The rock's bleak summit frowns above our head,
Looking immediate down, we almost fear
Lest some enormous fragment should descend
With hideous sweep into the vale, and crush
The intruding visitant. No sound is here,
Save of the stream that shrills, and now and then
A cry as of faint wailing, when the kite
Comes sailing o'er the crags, or straggling lamb
Bleats for its mother. Here, remote from man,
And life's discordant roar, might Piety
Lift up her early orisons to Him
Who made the world; who piled up, mighty rocks,
Your huge o'ershadowing summits; who devolved
The mighty rivers on their mazy course;
Who bade the seasons roll, and they rolled on
In harmony; who filled the earth with joy,
And spread it in magnificence. O GOD!
Thou also madest the great water-flood,
The deep that uttereth thy voice; whose waves
Toss fearful at thy bidding. Thou didst speak,
And lo! the great and glorious sun, from night
Tenfold upspringing, through the heavens' wide way
Held his untired career. These, in their course,
As with one shout of acclamation, praise
Thee, LORD! thee, FATHER! thee, ALMIGHTY KING!
Maker of earth and heaven! Nor less the flower
That shakes its purple head, and smiles unseen
Upon the mountain's van; nor less the stream
That tinkles through the cliff-encircled bourne,
Cheering with music the lone place, proclaim:
In wisdom, Father, hast thou made them all!
Scenes of retired sublimity, that fill
With fearful ecstasy and holy trance
The pausing mind! we leave your awful gloom,
And lo! the footway plank, that leads across
The narrow torrent, foaming through the chasm
Below; the rugged stones are washed and worn
Into a thousand shapes, and hollows scooped
By long attrition of the ceaseless surge,
Smooth, deep, and polished as the marble urn,
In their hard forms. Here let us sit, and watch
The struggling current burst its headlong way,
Hearing the noise it makes, and musing much
On the strange changes of this nether world.

How many ages must have swept to dust
The still succeeding multitudes, that "fret
Their little hour" upon this restless scene,
Or ere the sweeping waters could have cut
The solid rock so deep! As now its roar
Comes hollow from below, methinks we hear
The noise of generations, as they pass,
O'er the frail arch of earthly vanity,
To silence and oblivion. The loud coil
Ne'er ceases; as the running river sounds
From age to age, though each particular wave
That made its brief noise, as it hurried on,
Ev'n whilst we speak, is past, and heard no more;
So ever to the ear of Heaven ascends
The long, loud murmur of the rolling globe;
Its strife, its toils, its sighs, its shouts, the same!
But lo! upon the hilly croft, and scarce
Distinguished from the crags, the peasant hut
Forth peeping; nor unwelcome is the sight.
It seems to say: Though solitude be sweet,
And sweet are all the images that float
Like summer-clouds before the eye, and charm
The pensive wanderer's way, 'tis sweeter yet
To think that in this world a brother lives.
And lovelier smiles the scene, that, 'mid the wilds
Of rocks and mountains, the bemused thought
Remembers of humanity, and calls
The wildly-roving fancy back to life.
Here, then, I leave my harp, which I have touched
With careless hand, and here I bid farewell
To Fancy's fading pictures, and farewell
The ideal spirit that abides unseen
'Mid rocks, and woods, and solitudes. I hail
Rather the steps of Culture, that ascend
The precipice's side. She bids the wild
Bloom, and adorns with beauty not its own
The ridged mountain's tract; she speaks, and lo!
The yellow harvest nods upon the slope;
And through the dark and matted moss upshoots
The bursting clover, smiling to the sun.
These are thy offspring, Culture! the green herb
Is thine, that decks with rich luxuriance
The pasture's lawny range; the yellow corn,
That waves upon the upland ridge, is thine;
Thine too the elegant abode, that smiles
Amidst the rocky scene, and wakes the thought,
The tender thought, of all life's charities.
And senseless were my heart, could I look back

Upon the varied way my feet have trod,
Without a silent prayer that health and joy,
And love and happiness, may long abide
In the romantic vale where Ellen winds.

Coombe-Ellen (in Welsh, Cwm Elan) is situated among the most romantic mountains of Radnorshire, about five miles from Rhayd'r. This poem is inscribed to Thomas Grove, Esq. of Fern, Wiltshire, at whose summer residence, in Radnorshire, it was written.

SUMMER EVENING AT HOME

Come, lovely Evening! with thy smile of peace
Visit my humble dwelling; welcomed in,
Not with loud shouts, and the thronged city's din,
But with such sounds as bid all tumult cease
Of the sick heart; the grasshopper's faint pipe
Beneath the blades of dewy grass unripe,
The bleat of the lone lamb, the carol rude
Heard indistinctly from the village green,
The bird's last twitter, from the hedge-row seen,
Where, just before, the scattered crumbs I strewed,
To pay him for his farewell song;—all these
Touch soothingly the troubled ear, and please
The stilly-stirring fancies. Though my hours
(For I have drooped beneath life's early showers)
Pass lonely oft, and oft my heart is sad,
Yet I can leave the world, and feel most glad
To meet thee, Evening, here; here my own hand
Has decked with trees and shrubs the slopes around,
And whilst the leaves by dying airs are fanned,
Sweet to my spirit comes the farewell sound,
That seems to say: Forget the transient tear
Thy pale youth shed—Repose and Peace are here.

WINTER EVENING AT HOME

Fair Moon, that at the chilly day's decline
Of sharp December through my cottage pane
Dost lovely look, smiling, though in thy wane!
In thought, to scenes, serene and still as thine,
Wanders my heart, whilst I by turns survey
Thee slowly wheeling on thy evening way;
And this my fire, whose dim, unequal light,
Just glimmering, bids each shadowy image fall

Sombrous and strange upon the darkening wall,
Ere the clear tapers chase the deepening night!
Yet thy still orb, seen through the freezing haze,
Shines calm and clear without; and whilst I gaze,
I think, around me in this twilight room,
I but remark mortality's sad gloom;
Whilst hope and joy cloudless and soft appear,
In the sweet beam that lights thy distant sphere.

THE SPIRIT OF NAVIGATION

Stern Father of the storm! who dost abide
Amid the solitude of the vast deep,
For ever listening to the sullen tide,
And whirlwinds that the billowy desert sweep!
Thou at the distant death-shriek dost rejoice;
The rule of the tempestuous main is thine,
Outstretched and lone; thou utterest thy voice,
Like solemn thunders: These wild waves are mine;
Mine their dread empire; nor shall man profane
The eternal secrets of my ancient reign.

The voice is vain: secure, and as in scorn,
The gallant vessel scuds before the wind;
Her parting sails swell stately to the morn;
She leaves the green earth and its hills behind;
Gallant before the wind she goes, her prow
High bearing, and disparting the blue tide
That foams and flashes in its rage below;
Meantime the helmsman feels a conscious pride,
And while far onward the long billows swell,
Looks to the lessening land, that seems to say, Farewell!

Father of storms! then let thy whirlwinds roar
O'er seas of solitary amplitude;
Man, the poor tenant of thy rocky shore,
Man, thy terrific empire hath subdued;
And though thy waves toss his high-foundered bark
Where no dim watch-light gleams, still he defies
Thy utmost rage, and in his buoyant ark
Speeds on, regardless of the darkening skies;
And o'er the mountain-surges, as they roll,
Subdues his destined way, and speeds from pole to pole.

Behold him now, far from his native plain,
Where high woods shade some wild Hesperian bay,

Or green isles glitter in the southern main,
His streaming ensign to the morn display!
Behold him, where the North's pale meteors dance,
And icy rocks roll glimmering from afar,
Fearless through night and solitude advance!
Or where the pining sons of Andamar,
When dark eclipse has wrapt the labouring moon,
Howl to the demon of the dread monsoon!

Time was, like them, poor Nature's shivering child,
Pacing the beach, and by the salt spray beat,
He watched the melancholy surge, or smiled
To see it burn and bicker at his feet;
In some rude shaggy spot, by fortune placed,
He dreamed not of strange lands, and empires spread,
Beyond the rolling of the watery waste;
He saw the sun shine on the mountain's head,
But knew not, whilst he hailed the orient light,
What myriads blessed his beam, or sickened at the sight.

From some dark promontory, that o'erbent
The flashing waves, he heard their ceaseless roar;
Or carolled in his light canoe content,
As, bound from creek to creek, it grazed the shore;
Gods of the storm the dreary space might sweep,
And shapes of death, and gliding spectres gaunt,
Might flit, he thought, o'er the remoter deep;
And whilst strange voices cried, Avaunt, avaunt!
Uncertain lights, seen through the midnight gloom,
Might lure him sadly on to his cold watery tomb.

No city, then, amid the calm clear day,
O'er the blue waters' undulating line,
With battlements, and fans that glittered gay,
And piers, and thronging masts, was seen to shine.
No cheerful sounds were wafted on the gale,
Nor hummed the shores with early industry;
But mournful birds in hollow cliffs did wail,
And there all day the cormorant did cry,
While with sunk eye, and matted, dripping locks,
The houseless savage slept beneath the foam-beat rocks.

Thus slumbering long upon the dreamy verge
Of instinct, see, he rouses from his trance!
Faint, and as glimmering yet, the Arts emerge,
One after one, from darkness, and advance,
Beauteous, as o'er the heavens the stars' still way.
Now see the track of his dominion wide,

Fair smiling as the dayspring; cities gay
Lift their proud heads, and o'er the yellow tide,
Whilst sounds of fervent industry arise,
A thousand pennants float bright streaming in the skies!

Genius of injured Asia! once sublime
And glorious, now dim seen amid the storm,
And melancholy clouds of sweeping time,
Who yet dost half reveal thine awful form,
Pointing, with saddened aspect and slow hand,
To vast emporiums, desolate and waste;
To wrecks of unknown cities, sunk in sand!
'Twas at thy voice, Arts, Order, Science, Taste.
Upsprung, the East adorning, like the smile
Of Spring upon the banks of thy own swelling Nile.

'Twas at thy voice huge Enterprise awoke,
That, long on rocky Aradus reclined,
Slumbered to the hoarse surge that round her broke,
And hollow pipings of the idle wind;
She heard thy voice, upon the rock she stood
Gigantic, the rude scene she marked—she cried,
Let there be intercourse, and the great flood
Waft the rich plenty to these shores denied!
And soon thine eye delighted saw aspire,
Crowning the midland main, thy own Imperial Tyre.

Queen of the waters! who didst ope the gate
Of Commerce, and display in lands unknown
Thy venturous sail, ev'n now in ancient state
Methinks I see thee on thy rocky throne;
I see their massy piles thy cothons rear,
And on the deep a solemn shadow cast;
I traverse thy once echoing shores, and hear
The sound of mighty generations past:
I see thy kingly merchants' thronged resort,
And gold and purple gleam o'er all thy spacious port.

I mark thy glittering galleys sweep along—
The steady rowers to the strokes incline,
And chaunt in unison their choral song;
White through their oars the ivory benches shine;
The fine-wrought sails, which looms of Egypt wove,
Swell beautiful beneath the bending mast;
Hewn from proud Lebanon's immortal grove,
The oaks of Bashan brave the roaring blast!
So o'er the western wave thy vessels float,
For verdant Egypt bound, or Calpe's cliffs remote.

Queen of the waters! throned upon thy seat
Amid the sea, thy beauty and thy fame
The deep, that rolls low-murmuring at thy feet,
And all the multitude of isles, proclaim!
For thee Damascus piles her woolly store;
To thee their flocks Arabia's princes bring;
And Sheba heaps her spice and glittering ore;
The ships of Tarshish of thy glory sing:
Queen of the waters! who is like to thee,
Replenished in thy might, and throned on the sea!

The purple streamers fly, the trumpets sound,
The adventurous bark glides on in tranquil state;
The voyagers, with leafy garlands crowned,
Draw back their arms together, and elate
Sweep o'er the surge; the spray far scattered flies
Beneath the stroke of their unwearied oars;
To their loud shouts the circling coast replies;
And now, o'er the deep ocean, where it roars
They fly; till slowly lessening from the shore,
Beneath the haze they sink—sink, and are seen no more.

When Night descends, and with her silver bow
The Queen of Heaven comes forth in radiance bright,
Surveying the dim earth and seas below;
Why from afar resounds the mystic rite
Hymned round her uncouth altar? Virgins there
(Amid the brazen cymbal's hollow ring)
And aged priests the solemn feast prepare;
To her their nightly orisons they sing;
That she may look from her high throne, and guide
The wandering bark secure along the trackless tide.

Her on his nightly watch the pilot views
Careful, and by her soft and tranquil light,
Along the uncertain coast his track pursues;
And now he sees great Carmel's woody height,
Where nightly fires to grisly Baal burn;
Round the rough cape he winds; meantime far on
Thick eddying scuds the hollow surf upturn;
He thinks of the sweet light of summer gone!
He thinks, perhaps, dashed on the rugged shore,
He never shall behold his babes' loved mother more!

Slow comes the morn; but ah! what demon form,
While pealing thunder the high concave rends,
Rises more vast amid the rushing storm!

With dreadful shade his horrid bulk ascends
Dark to the driving clouds; beneath him roars
The deep; his troubled brow is wrapped in gloom;
See, it moves onwards; now more huge it soars!
Who shall avert the poor seafarer's doom!
Who now shall save him from the spectre's might
That treads the rocking waves in thunder and in night!

Dread phantom! art thou he whose fearful sway,
As Egypt's hoary chronicles have told,
The clouds, the whirlwinds, and the seas obey,
Typhon, of aspect hideous to behold!
Oh, spare the wretched wanderers, who, led
By flattering hopes, have left the peaceful shore!
Behold, they shrink, they bend with speechless dread;
From their faint grasp drops the unheeded oar!
It answers not, but mingling seas and sky,
In clouds, and wind, and thunder, rushes by.

Hail to thy light, lord of the golden day,
That, bursting through the sable clouds again,
Dost cheer the seaman's solitary way,
And with new splendour deck the lucid main!
And lo! the voyage past, where many a palm,
Its green top only seen, the prospect bounds,
Fringing the sunny sea-line, clear and calm;
Now hark the slowly-swelling human sounds!
Meantime the bark along the placid bay
Of Tamiatis keeps her easy-winding way.

Here rest we safe from scenes of peril past,
No danger lurks in this serene retreat;
No more is heard the roaring of the blast,
But pastoral sounds of scattered flocks that bleat,
Or evening herds that o'er the champaign low;
Here citrons tall and purple dates around
Delicious fragrance and cool shade bestow;
The shores with murmuring industry resound;
While through the vernal pastures where he strays,
The Nile, as with delight, his mazy course delays.

WATER-PARTY ON BEAULIEU RIVER, IN THE NEW FOREST

I thought 'twas a toy of the fancy, a dream
That leads with illusion the senses astray,
And I sighed with delight as we stole down the stream,

While the sun, as he smiled on our sail, seemed to say,
Rejoice in my light, ere it fade fast away!

We left the loud rocking of ocean behind,
And stealing along the clear current serene,
The Phædria spread her white sails to the wind,
And they who divided had many a day been,
Gazed with added delight on the charms of the scene.

Each bosom one spirit of peace seemed to feel;
We heard not the tossing, the stir, and the roar
Of the ocean without; we heard only the keel,
The keel that went whispering along the green shore,
And the stroke, as it dipped, of the feathering oar.

Beneath the dark woods now, as winding we go,
What sounds of rich harmony burst on the ear!
Hark, cheer'ly the loud-swelling clarionets blow;
Now the tones gently die, now more mellow we hear
The horns through the high forest echoing clear!

They cease; and no longer the echoes prolong
The swell of the concert; in silence we float—
In silence! Oh, listen! 'tis woman's sweet song—
The bends of the river reply to each note,
And the oar is held dripping and still from the boat.

Mark the sun that descends o'er the curve of the flood!
Seize, Wilmot, the pencil, and instant convey
To the tablet the water, the banks, and the wood,
That their colours may live without change or decay,
When these beautiful tints die in darkness away.

So when we are parted, and tossed on the deep,
And no longer the light on our prospect shall gleam,
The semblance of one lovely scene we may keep,
And remember the day, and the hour, like a dream,
When we sighed with delight as we stole down the stream!

MONODY ON THE DEATH OF DR WARTON

Oh! I should ill thy generous cares requite
Thou who didst first inspire my timid Muse,
Could I one tuneful tear to thee refuse,
Now that thine aged eyes are closed in night,
Kind Warton! Thou hast stroked my stripling head,

And sometimes, mingling soft reproof with praise,
My path hast best directed through the maze
Of thorny life: by thee my steps were led
To that romantic valley, high o'erhung
With sable woods, where many a minstrel rung
His bold harp to the sweeping waterfall;
Whilst Fancy loved around each form to call
That fill the poet's dream: to this retreat
Of Fancy, (won by whose enticing lay
I have forgot how sunk the summer's day),
Thou first did guide my not unwilling feet;
Meantime inspiring the gay breast of youth
With love of taste, of science, and of truth.
The first inciting sounds of human praise,
A parent's love excepted, came from thee;
And but for thee, perhaps, my boyish days
Had all passed idly, and whate'er in me
Now live of hope, been buried.
I was one,
Long bound by cold dejection's numbing chain,
As in a torpid trance, that deemed it vain
To struggle; nor my eyelids to the sun
Uplifted: but I heard thy cheering voice;
I shook my deadly slumber off; I gazed
Delighted 'round; awaked, inspired, amazed,
I marked another world, and in my choice
Lovelier, and decked with light! On fairy ground
Methought I buoyant trod, and heard the sound
As of enchanting melodies, that stole,
Stole gently, and entranced my captive soul.
Then all was life and hope! 'Twas thy first ray,
Sweet Fancy, on the heart; as when the day
Of Spring, along the melancholy tract
Of wintry Lapland, dawns; the cataract,
From ice dissolving on the silent side
Of some white precipice, with paly gleam
Descends, while the cold hills a slanting beam
Faint tinges: till, ascending in his pride,
The great Sun from the red horizon looks,
And wakes the tuneless birds, the stagnant brooks,
And sleeping lakes! So on my mind's cold night
The ray of Fancy shone, and gave delight
And hope past utterance.
Thy cheering voice,
O Warton! bade my silent heart rejoice,
And wake to love of nature; every breeze,
On Itchin's brink was melody; the trees
Waved in fresh beauty; and the wind and rain,

That shook the battlements of Wykeham's fane,
Not less delighted, when, with random pace,
I trod the cloistered aisles; and witness thou,
Catherine, upon whose foss-encircled brow
We met the morning, how I loved to trace
The prospect spread around; the rills below,
That shone irriguous in the gleaming plain;
The river's bend, where the dark barge went slow,
And the pale light on yonder time-worn fane!
So passed my days with new delight; mean time
To Learning's tender eye thou didst unfold
The classic page, and what high bards of old,
With solemn notes, and minstrelsy sublime,
Have chanted, we together heard; and thou,
Warton! wouldst bid me listen, till a tear
Sprang to mine eye: now the bold song we hear
Of Greece's sightless master-bard: the breast
Beats high; with stern Pelides to the plain
We rush; or o'er the corpse of Hector slain
Hang pitying;—and lo! where pale, oppressed
With age and grief, sad Priam comes; with beard
All white he bows, kissing the hands besmeared
With his last hope's best blood!
The oaten reed
Now from the mountain sounds; the sylvan Muse,
Reclined by the clear stream of Arethuse,
Wakes the Sicilian pipe; the sunny mead
Swarms with the bees, whose drowsy lullaby
Soothes the reclining ox with half-closed eye;
While in soft cadence to the madrigal,
From rock to rock the whispering waters fall!
But who is he, that, by yon gloomy cave,
Bids heaven and earth bear witness to his woe!
And hark! how hollowly the ocean-wave
Echoes his plaint, and murmurs deep below!
Haste, let the tall ship stem the tossing tide,
That he may leave his cave, and hear no more
The Lemnian surges unrejoicing roar;
And be great Fate through the dark world thy guide,
Sad Philoctetes!
So Instruction bland,
With young-eyed Sympathy, went hand in hand
O'er classic fields; and let my heart confess
Its holier joy, when I essayed to climb
The lonely heights where Shakspeare sat sublime,
Lord of the mighty spell: around him press
Spirits and fairy-forms. He, ruling wide
His visionary world, bids terror fill

The shivering breast, or softer pity thrill
Ev'n to the inmost heart. Within me died
All thoughts of this low earth, and higher powers
Seemed in my soul to stir; till, strained too long,
The senses sunk.
Then, Ossian, thy wild song
Haply beguiled the unheeded midnight hours,
And, like the blast that swept Berrathron's towers,
Came pleasant and yet mournful to my soul!
See o'er the autumnal heath the gray mists roll!
Hark to the dim ghosts' faint and feeble cry,
As on the cloudy tempest they pass by!
Saw ye huge Loda's spectre-shape advance,
Through which the stars look pale!
Nor ceased the trance
Which bound the erring fancy, till dark night
Flew silent by, and at my window-grate
The morning bird sang loud: nor less delight
The spirit felt, when still and charmed I sate
Great Milton's solemn harmonies to hear,
That swell from the full chord, and strong and clear,
Beyond the tuneless couplets' weak control,
Their long-commingling diapason roll,
In varied sweetness.
Nor, amidst the choir
Of pealing minstrelsy, was thy own lyre,
Warton, unheard;—as Fancy poured the song,
The measured music flowed along,
Till all the heart and all the sense
Felt her divinest influence,
In throbbing sympathy:—Prepare the car,
And whirl us, goddess, to the war,
Where crimson banners fire the skies,
Where the mingled shouts arise,
Where the steed, with fetlock red,
Tramples the dying and the dead;
And amain, from side to side,
Death his pale horse is seen to ride!
Or rather, sweet enthusiast, lead
Our footsteps to the cowslip mead,
Where, as the magic spell is wound,
Dying music floats around:—
Or seek we some gray ruin's shade,
And pity the cold beggar, laid
Beneath the ivy-rustling tower,
At the dreary midnight hour,
Scarce sheltered from the drifting snow;
While her dark locks the bleak winds blow

O'er her sleeping infant's cheek!
Then let the shrilling trumpet speak,
And pierce in louder tones the ear,
Till, while it peals, we seem to hear
The sounding march, as of the Theban's song;
And varied numbers, in their course,
With gathering fulness, and collected force,
Like the broad cataract, swell and sweep along!
Struck by the sounds, what wonder that I laid,
As thou, O Warton! didst the theme inspire,
My inexperienced hand upon the lyre,
And soon with transient touch faint music made,
As soon forgotten!
So I loved to lie
By the wild streams of elfin poesy,
Rapt in strange musings; but when life began,
I never roamed a visionary man;
For, taught by thee, I learned with sober eyes
To look on life's severe realities.
I never made (a dream-distempered thing)
Poor Fiction's realm my world; but to cold Truth
Subdued the vivid shapings of my youth.
Save when the drisly woods were murmuring,
Or some hard crosses had my spirit bowed;
Then I have left, unseen, the careless crowd,
And sought the dark sea roaring, or the steep
That braved the storm; or in the forest deep,
As all its gray leaves rustled, wooed the tone
Of the loved lyre, that, in my springtide gone,
Waked me to transport.
Eighteen summers now
Have smiled on Itchin's margin, since the time
When these delightful visions of our prime
Rose on my view in loveliness. And thou
Friend of my muse, in thy death-bed art cold,
Who, with the tenderest touches, didst unfold
The shrinking leaves of Fancy, else unseen
And shelterless: therefore to thee are due
Whate'er their summer sweetness; and I strew,
Sadly, such flowerets as on hillocks green,
Or mountain-slope, or hedge-row, yet my hand
May cull, with many a recollection bland,
And mingled sorrow, Warton, on thy tomb,
To whom, if bloom they boast, they owe their bloom!

EPITAPH ON H. WALMSLEY, ESQ., IN ALVERSTOKE CHURCH, HANTS

Oh! they shall ne'er forget thee, they who knew
Thy soul benevolent, sincere, and true;
The poor thy kindness cheered, thy bounty fed,
Whom age left shivering in its dreariest shed;
Thy friends, who sorrowing saw thee, when disease
Seemed first the genial stream of life to freeze,
Pale from thy hospitable home depart,
Thy hand still open, and yet warm thy heart!
But how shall she her love, her loss express,
Thy widow, in this uttermost distress,
When she with anguish hears her lisping train
Upon their buried father call in vain!
She wipes the tear despair had forced to flow,
She lifts her look beyond this vale of woe,
And rests (while humbled in the dust she kneels)
On Him who only knows how much she feels.

AGE

Age, thou the loss of health and friends shalt mourn!
But thou art passing to that night-still bourne,
Where labour sleeps. The linnet, chattering loud
To the May morn, shall sing; thou, in thy shroud,
Forgetful and forgotten, sink to rest;
And grass-green be the sod upon thy breast!

ON A LANDSCAPE BY RUBENS

Nay, let us gaze, ev'n till the sense is full,
Upon the rich creation, shadowed so
That not great Nature, in her loftiest pomp
Of living beauty, ever on the sight
Rose more magnificent; nor aught so fair
Hath Fancy, in her wildest, brightest mood,
Imaged of things most lovely, when the sounds
Of this cold cloudy world at distance sink,
And all alone the warm idea lives
Of what is great, or beautiful, or good,
In Nature's general plan.

So the vast scope,
O Rubens! of thy mighty mind, and such
The fervour of thy pencil, pouring wide

The still illumination, that the mind
Pauses, absorbed, and scarcely thinks what powers
Of mortal art the sweet enchantment wrought.
She sees the painter, with no human touch,
Create, embellish, animate at will,
The mimic scenes, from Nature's ampler range
Caught as by inspiration; while the clouds,
High wandering, and the fairest form of things,
Seem at his bidding to emerge, and burn
With radiance and with life!

Let us, subdued,
Now to the magic of the moment lose
The thoughts of life, and mingle every sense
Ev'n in the scenes before us!
The fresh morn
Of summer shines; the white clouds of the east
Are crisped; beneath, the bright blue champaign steams;
The banks, the meadows, and the flowers, send up
An incensed exhalation, like the meek
And holy praise of Him whose soul's deep joy
The lone woods witness. Thou, whose heart is sick
Of vanities; who, in the throng of men,
Dost feel no lenient fellowship; whose eye
Turns, with a languid carelessness, around
Upon the toiling crowd, still murmuring on,
Restless;—oh, think, in summer scenes like these,
How sweet the sense of quiet gladness is,
That, like the silent breath of morning, steals
From lowly nooks, and feels itself expand
Amid the works of Nature, to the Power
That made them: to the awful thought of HIM
Who, when the morning stars shouted for joy,
Bade the great sun from tenfold darkness burst,
The green earth roll in light, and solitude
First hear the voice of man, whilst hills and woods
Stood eminent, in orient hues arrayed,
His dwelling; and all living Nature smiled,
As in this pictured semblance, beaming full
Before us!

Mark again the various view:
Some city's far-off spires and domes appear,
Breaking the long horizon, where the morn
Sits blue and soft: what glowing imagery
Is spread beneath!—Towns, villages, light smoke,
And scarce-seen windmill-sails, and devious woods,
Chequering 'mid sunshine the grass-level land,

That stretches from the sight.

Now nearer trace
The forms of trees distinct—the broad brown oak;
The poplars, that, with silvery trunks, incline,
Shading the lonely castle; flakes of light
Are flung behind the massy groups, that, now
Enlarging and enlarging still, unfold
Their separate beauties. But awhile delay;
Pass the foot-bridge, and listen (for we hear,
Or think we hear her), listen to the song
Of yonder milkmaid, as she brims her pail;
Whilst, in the yellow pasture, pensive near,
The red cows ruminate.
Break off, break off, for lo! where, all alarmed,
The small birds, from the late resounding perch,
Fly various, hushed their early song; and mark,
Beneath the darkness of the bramble-bank
That overhangs the half-seen brook, where nod
The flowing rushes, dew-besprent, with breast
Ruddy, and emerald wing, the kingfisher
Steals through the dripping sedge away. What shape
Of terrors scares the woodland habitants,
Marring the music of the dawn? Look round;
See, where he creeps, beneath the willowy stump,
Cowering and low, step silent after step,
The booted fowler: keen his look, and fixed
Upon the adverse bank, while, with firm hand,
He grasps the deadly tube; his dog, with ears
Hung back, and still and steady eye of fire,
Points to the prey; the boor, intent, moves on
Panting, and creeping close beneath the leaves,
And fears lest ev'n the rustling reeds betray
His footfall; nearer yet, and yet more near,
He stalks. Who now shall save the heedless group,
The speckled partridges, that in the sun,
On yonder hillock green, across the stream,
Bask unalarmed beneath the hawthorn bush,
Whose aged boughs the crawling blackberry
Entwines!

And thus, upon the sweetest scenes
Of human loveliness, and social peace
Domestic, when the full fond heart reclines
Upon its hopes, and almost mingles tears
Of joy, to think that in this hollow world
Such bliss should be its portion; then (alas,
The bitter change!), then, with his unheard step,

In darkness shrouded, yet approaching fast,
Death, from amidst the sunny flowers, lifts up
His giant dread anatomy, and smites,
Smites the fair prospect once, whilst every bloom
Hangs shrivelled, and a sound of mourning fills
The lone and blasted valley: but no sound
Is here of sorrow or of death, though she,
The country Kate, with shining morning cheek
(Who, in the tumbril, with her market-gear,
Sits seated high), seems to expect the flash
Exploding, that shall lay the innocent
And feathered tenants of the landscape low.
Not so the clown, who, heedless whether life
Or death betide, across the plashy ford
Drives slow; the beasts plod on, foot following foot,
Aged and grave, with half-erected ears,
As now his whip above their matted manes
Hangs tremulous, while the dark and shallow stream
Flashes beneath their fetlock: he, astride
On harness saddle, not a sidelong look
Deigns at the breathing landscape, or the maid
Smiling behind; the cold and lifeless calf
Her sole companion: and so mated oft
Is some sweet maid, whose thrilling heart was formed
For dearer fellowship. But lift the eye,
And hail the abode of rural ease. The man
Walks forth, from yonder antique hall, that looks
The mistress of the scene; its turrets gleam
Amid the trees, and cheerful smoke is seen,
As if no spectred shape (though most retired
The spot) there ever wandered, stoled in white,
Along the midnight chambers; but quaint Mab
Her tiny revels led, till the rare dawn
Peeped out, and chanticleer his shrill alarm
Beneath the window rang, then, with a wink,
The shadowy rout have vanished!
As the morn
Jocund ascends, how lovely is the view
To him who owns the fair domain! The friend
Of his still hours is near, to whom he vowed
His truth; her eyes reflect his bliss; his heart
Beats high with joy; his little children play,
Pleased, in his pathway; one the scattered flowers
Straggling collects, the other spreads its arms,
In speechless blandishment, upon the neck
Of its caressing nurse.

Still let us gaze,

And image every form of heartfelt joy
Which scenes like these bestow, that charm the sight,
Yet soothe the spirit. All is quiet here,
Yet cheerful as the green sea, when it shines
In some still bay, shines in its loneliness
Beneath the breeze, that moves, and hardly moves,
The placid surface.

On the balustrade
Of the old bridge, that o'er the moat is thrown,
The fisher with his angle leans intent,
And turns, from the bright pomp of spreading plains,
To watch the nimble fry, that glancing oft
Beneath the gray arch shoot! Oh, happiest he
Who steals through life, untroubled as unseen!
The distant city, with its crowded spires,
That dimly shines upon his view, awakes
No thought but that of pleasure more composed,
As the winds whisper him to sounder sleep.
He leans upon the faithful arm of her
For whom his youthful heart beat, fondly beat,
When life was new: time steals away, yet health
And exercise are his; and in these shades,
Though sometimes he has mourned a proud world's wrong,
He feels an independence that all cares
Breasts with a carol of content; he hears
The green leaves of his old paternal trees
Make music, soothing as they stir: the elm,
And poplar with its silvery trunk, that shades
The green sward of the bank before his porch,
Are to him as companions;—whilst he turns
With more endearment to the living smile
Of those his infants, who, when he is dead,
Shall hear the music of the self-same trees
Waving, till years roll on, and their gray hairs
Go to the dust in peace.

Away, sad thought!
Lo! where the morning light, through the dark wood,
Upon the window-pane is flung like fire,
Hail, Life and Hope; and thou, great work of art,
That 'mid this populous and busy swarm
Of men dost smile serene, as with the hues
Of fairest, grandest Nature; may'st thou speak
Not vainly of the endearments and best joys
That Nature yields. The manliest heart that swells
With honest English feelings,—while the eye,
Saddened, but not cast down, beholds far off

The darkness of the onward rolling storm,—
Charmed for a moment by this mantling view,
Its anxious tumults shall suspend: and such,
The pensive patriot shall exclaim, thy scenes,
My own beloved country, such the abode
Of rural peace! and while the soul has warmth,
And voice has energy, the brave arm strength,
England, thou shalt not fall! The day shall come,
Yes, and now is, that thou shalt lift thyself;
And woe to him who sets upon thy shores
His hostile foot! Proud victor though he be,
His bloody march shall never soil a flower
That hangs its sweet head, in the morning dew,
On thy green village banks! His mustered hosts
Shall be rolled back in thousands, and the surge
Bury them! Then, when peace illumes once more,
My country, thy green nooks and inmost vales,
It will be sweet amidst the forest glens
To stray, and think upon the distant storm
That howled, but injured not!

At thoughts like these,
What heart, what English heart, but shall beat high!
Meantime, its keen flash passed, thine eye intent,
Beaumont, shall trace the master-strokes of art,
And view the assemblage of the finished piece,
As with his skill who formed it: ruder views,
Savage, with solitary pines, hung high
Amid the broken crags (where scowling wait
The fierce banditti), stern Salvator's hand
Shall aptly shade: o'er Poussin's clustering domes,
With ampler umbrage, the black woods shall hang,
Beneath whose waving gloom the sudden flash
Of broken light upon the brawling stream
Is flung below.

Aërial Claude shall paint
The gray fane peering o'er the summer woods,
The azure lake below, or distant seas,
And sails, in the pellucid atmosphere,
Soft gleaming to the morn. Dark on the rock,
Where the red lightnings burst, shall Wilson stand,
Like mighty Shakspeare, whom the imps of fire
Await. Nor oh, sweet Gainsborough! shall thee
The Muse forget, whose simple landscape smiles
Attractive, whether we delight to view
The cottage chimney through the high wood peep;
Or beggar beauty stretch her little hand,

With look most innocent; or homeward kine
Wind through the hollow road at eventide,
Or browse the straggling branches.

Scenes like these
Shall charm all hearts, while truth and beauty live,
And Nature's pictured loveliness shall own
Each master's varied touch; but chiefly thou,
Great Rubens! shalt the willing senses lead,
Enamoured of the varied imagery,
That fills the vivid canvas, swelling still
On the enraptured eye of taste, and still
New charms unfolding; though minute, yet grand,
Simple, yet most luxuriant; every light
And every shade, greatly opposed, and all
Subserving to one magical effect
Of truth and harmony.

So glows the scene;
And to the pensive thought refined displays
The richest rural poem. Oh, may views
So pictured animate thy classic mind,
Beaumont, to wander 'mid Sicilian scenes,
And catch the beauties of the pastoral bard,
Shadowing his wildest landscapes! Ætna's fires,
Bebrycian rocks, Anapus' holy stream,
And woods of ancient Pan; the broken crag
And the old fisher here; the purple vines
There bending; and the smiling boy set down
To guard, who, innocent and happy, weaves,
Intent, his rushy basket, to ensnare
The chirping grasshoppers, nor sees the while
The lean fox meditate her morning meal,
Eyeing his scrip askance; whilst further on
Another treads the purple grapes—he sits,
Nor aught regards, but the green rush he weaves.
O Beaumont! let this pomp of light and shade
Wake thee, to paint the woods that the sweet Muse
Has consecrated: then the summer scenes
Of Phasidamus, clad in richer light,
Shall glow, the glancing poplars, and clear fount;
While distant times admire (as now we trace
This summer-mantling view) hoar Ætna's pines,
The vine-hung grotts, and branching planes, that shade
The silver Arethusa's stealing wave.

THE HARP, AND DESPAIR, OF COWPER

Sweet bard, whose tones great Milton might approve,
And Shakspeare, from high Fancy's sphere,
Turning to the sound his ear,
Bend down a look of sympathy and love;
Oh, swell the lyre again,
As if in full accord it poured an angel's strain!
But oh! what means that look aghast,
Ev'n whilst it seemed in holy trance,
On scenes of bliss above to glance!
Was it a fiend of darkness passed!
Oh, speak—
Paleness is upon his cheek—
On his brow the big drops stand,
To airy vacancy
Points the dread silence of his eye,
And the loved lyre it falls, falls from his nerveless hand!
Come, peace of mind, delightful guest!
Oh, come, and make thy downy nest
Once more on his sad heart!
Meek Faith, a drop of comfort shed;
Sweet Hope, support his aged head;
And Charity, avert the burning dart!
Fruitless the prayer—the night of deeper woes
Seems o'er the head even now to close;
In vain the path of purity he trod,
In vain, in vain,
He poured from Fancy's shell his sweetest hermit strain—
He has no hope on earth: forsake him not, O God!

STANZAS FOR MUSIC

I trust the happy hour will come,
That shall to peace thy breast restore;
And that we two, beloved friend,
Shall one day meet to part no more.

It grieves me most, that parting thus,
All my soul feels I dare not speak;
And when I turn me from thy sight,
The tears in silence wet my cheek.

Yet I look forward to the time,
That shall each wound of sorrow heal;
When I may press thee to my heart,

And tell thee all that now I feel.e

MUSIC

O Music! if thou hast a charm
That may the sense of pain disarm,
Be all thy tender tones addressed
To soothe to peace my Harriet's breast;
And bid the magic of thy strain
So still the wakeful throb of pain,
That, rapt in the delightful measure,
Sweet Hope again may whisper pleasure,
And seem the notes of Spring to hear,
Prelusive to a happier year!
And if thy magic can restore
The shade of days that smile no more,
And softer, sweeter colours give
To scenes that in remembrance live;
Be to her pensive heart a friend,
And, whilst the tender shadows blend,
Recall, ere the brief trace be lost,
Each moment that she prized the most.
Perhaps, when many a cheerful day
Hereafter shall have stolen away,
If then some old and favourite strain
Should bring back to her thoughts again
The hours when, silent by her side,
I listened to her song and sighed;
Perhaps a long-forgotten name,
A thought, if not a tear may claim;
And when in distant plains away,
Alone I count each lingering day,
She may a silent prayer prefer
For him whose heart once bled for her.

ABSENCE

OCTOBER

How shall I cheat the heavy hours, of thee
Deprived, of thy kind looks and converse sweet,
Now that the waving grove the dark storms beat,
And wintry winds sad sounding o'er the lea,
Scatter the sallow leaf! I would believe,
Thou, at this hour, with tearful tenderness

Dost muse on absent images, and press
In thought my hand, and say: Oh do not grieve,
Friend of my heart! at wayward fortune's power;
One day we shall be happy, and each hour
Of pain forget, cheered by the summer ray.
These thoughts beguile my sorrow for thy loss,
And, as the aged pines their dark heads toss,
Oft steal the sense of solitude away.
So am I sadly soothed, yet do I cast
A wishful glance upon the seasons past,
And think how different was the happy tide,
When thou, with looks of love, wert smiling by my side.

FAIRY SKETCH

SCENE—NETLEY ABBEY

There was a morrice on the moonlight plain,
And music echoed in the woody glade,
For fay-like forms, as of Titania's train,
Upon a summer eve, beneath the shade
Of Netley's ivied ruins, to the sound
Of sprightly minstrelsy did beat the ground:—
Come, take hands! and lightly move,
While our boat, in yonder cove,
Rests upon the darkening sea;
Come, take hands, and follow me!

Netley! thy dim and desolated fane
Hath heard, perhaps, the spirits of the night
Shrieking, at times, amid the wind and rain;
Or haply, when the full-orbed moon shone bright,
Thy glimmering aisles have echoed to the song
Of fairy Mab, who led her shadowy masque along.
Now, as to the sprightly sound
Of moonlight minstrelsy we beat the ground;
From the pale nooks, in accent clear,
Now, methinks, her voice I hear,
Sounding o'er the darksome sea;
Come, take hands, and follow me!

Here, beneath the solemn wood,
When faintly-blue is all the sky,
And the moon is still on high,
To the murmurs of the flood,
To the glimpses of the night,

We perform our airy rite;—
Care and pain to us unknown,
To the darkening seas are flown.

Hear no more life's fretful noise,
Heed not here pale Envy's sting,
Far from life's distempered joys;
To the waters murmuring,
To the shadows of the sky,
To the moon that rides on high,
To the glimpses of the night,
We perform our airy rite,
While care and pain, to us unknown,
To the darkening seas are flown.

INSCRIPTION

Come, and where these runnels fall,
Listen to my madrigal!
Far from all sounds of all the strife,
That murmur through the walks of life;
From grief, inquietude, and fears,
From scenes of riot, or of tears;
From passions, cankering day by day,
That wear the inmost heart away;
From pale Detraction's envious spite,
That worries where it fears to bite;
From mad Ambition's worldly chase,
Come, and in this shady place,
Be thine Contentment's humble joys,
And a life that makes no noise,
Save when fancy, musing long,
Turns to desultory song;
And wakes some lonely melody,
Like the water dripping by.
Come, and where these runnels fall,
Listen to my madrigal!

PICTURES FROM THEOCRITUS

FROM IDYL I

Greek: Ady ti to psthyrisma, etc.

Goat-herd, how sweet above the lucid spring

The high pines wave with breezy murmuring!
So sweet thy song, whose music might succeed
To the wild melodies of Pan's own reed.

THYRSIS

More sweet thy pipe's enchanting melody
Than streams that fall from broken rocks on high.
Say, by the nymphs, that guard the sacred scene,
Where lowly tamarisks shade these hillocks green,
At noontide shall we lie?
No; for o'erwearied with the forest chase,
Pan, the great hunter god, sleeps in this place.
Beneath the branching elm, while thy sad verse,
O Thyrsis! Daphnis' sorrows shall rehearse,
Fronting the wood-nymph's solitary seat,
Whose fountains flash amid the dark retreat;
Where the old statue leans, and brown oaks wave
Their ancient umbrage o'er the pastoral cave;
There will we rest, and thou, as erst, prolong
The sweet enchantment of the Doric song!

FROM THE SAME IDYL

Mark, where the beetling precipice appears,
The toil of the old fisher, gray with years;
Mark, as to drag the laden net he strains,
The labouring muscle and the swelling veins!
There, in the sun, the clustered vineyard bends,
And shines empurpled, as the morn ascends!
A little boy, with idly-happy mien,
To guard the grapes upon the ground is seen;
Two wily foxes creeping round appear,—
The scrip that holds his morning meal is near,—
One breaks the bending vines; with longing lip,
And look askance, one eyes the tempting scrip.
He plats and plats his rushy net all day,
And makes the vagrant grasshopper his prey;
He plats his net, intent with idle care,
Nor heeds how vineyard, grape, or scrip may fare.

FROM THE SAME

Where were ye, nymphs, when Daphnis drooped with love?
In fair Peneus' Tempe, or the grove
Of Pindus! Nor your pastimes did ye keep,
Where huge Anapus' torrent waters sweep;
On Ætna's height, ah! impotent to save,

Nor yet where Akis winds his holy wave!

FROM THE SAME

Pan, Pan, oh mighty hunter! whether now,
Thou roamest o'er Lyceus' shaggy brow,
Or Moenalaus, outstretched in amplest shade,
Thy solitary footsteps have delayed;
Leave Helice's romantic rock a while,
And haste, oh haste, to the Sicilian isle;
Leave the dread monument, approached with fear,
That Lycaonian tomb the gods revere.
Here cease, Sicilian Muse, the Doric lay;—
Come, Forest King, and bear this pipe away;
Daphnis, subdued by love, and bowed with woe,
Sinks, sinks for ever to the shades below.

FROM IDYL VII

He left us;—we, the hour of parting come,
To Prasidamus' hospitable home,
Myself and Eucritus, together wend,
With young Amynticus, our blooming friend:
There, all delighted, through the summer day,
On beds of rushes, pillowed deep, we lay;
Around, the lentils, newly cut, were spread;
Dark elms and poplars whispered o'er our head;
A hallowed stream, to all the wood-nymphs dear,
Fresh from the rocky cavern murmured near;
Beneath the fruit-leaves' many-mantling shade,
The grasshoppers a coil incessant made;
From the wild thorny thickets, heard remote,
The wood-lark trilled his far-resounding note;
Loud sung the thrush, musician of the scene,
And soft and sweet was heard the dove's sad note between;
Then yellow bees, whose murmur soothed the ear,
Went idly flitting round the fountain clear.
Summer and Autumn seemed at once to meet,
Filling with redolence the blest retreat,
While the ripe pear came rolling to our feet.

FROM IDYL XXII

When the famed Argo now secure had passed
The crushing rocks, and that terrific strait
That guards the wintry Pontic, the tall ship
Reached wild Bebrycia's shores; bearing like gods
Her god-descended chiefs. They, from her sides,

With scaling steps descend, and on the shore,
Savage, and sad, and beat by ocean winds,
Strewed their rough beds, and on the casual fire
The vessels place. The brothers, by themselves,
CASTOR and red-haired POLLUX, wander far
Into the forest solitudes. A wood
Immense and dark, shagging the mountain side,
Before them rose; a cold and sparkling fount
Welled with perpetual lapse, beneath its feet,
Of purest water clear; scattering below,
Streams as of silver and of crystal rose,
Bright from the bottom: Pines, of stateliest height,
Poplar, and plane, and cypress, branching wide,
Were near, thick bordered by the scented flowers
That lured the honeyed bee, when spring declines,
Thick swarming o'er the meadows. There all day
A huge man sat, of savage, wild aspect;
His breast stood roundly forward, his broad back
Seemed as of iron, such as might befit
A vast Colossus sculptured. Full to view
The muscles of his brawny shoulders stood,
Like the round mountain-stones the torrent wave
Has polished; from his neck and back hung down
A lion's skin, held by its claws. Him first
The red-haired youth addressed: Hail, stranger, hail,
And say, what tribes unknown inhabit here!
Take to the seas thy Hail: I ask it not,
Who never saw before, or thee, or thine.
Courage! thou seest not men that are unjust
Or cruel.
Courage shall I learn from thee!
Thy heart is savage; thou art passion's slave.
Such as I am thou seest; but land of thine
I tread not.
Come, these hospitable gifts
Accept, and part in peace.
No: not from thee.
My gifts are yet in store.
Say, may we drink
Of this clear fount?
Ask, when wan thirst has parched
Thy lips.
What present shall I give to thee?
None. Stand before me as a man; lift high
Thy brandished arms, and try, weak pugilist,
Thy strength.
But say, with whom shall I contend?
Thou seest him here; nor in his art unskilled.

Then what shall be the prize of him who wins?
Or thou shalt be my slave, or I be thine.
The crested birds so fight.
Whether like birds
Or lions, for no other prize fight we!
He said: and sounded loud his hollow conch;
The gaunt Bebrycian brethren, at the sound,
With long lank hair, come flocking to the shade
Of that vast plain.
Then Castor hied, and called
The hero chiefs from the Magnesian ship.

SKETCHES IN THE EXHIBITION

What various objects strike with various force,
Achilles, Hebe, and Sir Watkin's horse!
Here summer scenes, there Pentland's stormy ridge,
Lords, ladies, Noah's ark, and Cranford bridge!
Some that display the elegant design,
The lucid colours, and the flowing line;
Some that might make, alas! Walsh Porter stare,
And wonder how the devil they got there!

LADY M——VE

How clear a strife of light and shade is spread!
The face how touched with nature's loveliest red!
The eye, how eloquent, and yet how meek!
The glow subdued, yet mantling on thy cheek!
M——ve! I mark alone thy beauteous face,
But all is nature, dignity, and grace!

HON. MISS MERCER.—HOPNER

Oh! hide those tempting eyes, that faultless form,
Those looks with feeling and with nature warm;
The neck, the softly-swelling bosom hide,
Nor, wanton gales, blow the light vest aside;
For who, when beauties more than life excite
Silent applause, can gaze without delight!
But innocence, enchanting maid, is thine;
Thine eyes in liquid light unconscious shine;
And may thy breast no other feelings prove,
Than those of sympathy and mutual love!

SKETCHES IN THE EXHIBTION 1807

BLIND FIDDLER.—WILKIE

With mirth unfeigned the cottage chimney rings,
Though only vocal with four fiddle-strings:
And see, the poor blind fiddler draws his bow,
And lifts intent his time-denoting toe;
While yonder maid, as blythe as birds in June,
You almost hear her whistle to the tune!
Hard by, a lad, in imitative guise,
Fixed, fiddle-like, the broken bellows plies;
Before the hearth, with looks of honest joy,
The father chirrups to the chattering boy,
And snaps his lifted thumbs with mimic glee,
To the glad urchin on his mother's knee!

MORNING.—TURNER

Up! for the morning shines with welcome ray,
And to the sunny seabeach let us stray.
What orient hues proclaim the master's hand!
How light the wave upon the half-wet sand!
How beautiful the sun, as still we gaze,
Streams all diffusive through the opening haze!
Artist—when to the thunder's pealing sound,
Fire mixed with hailstones ran upon the ground,
When partial darkness the dread prospect hid,
And sole aspired the aged pyramid—
Sublimity thy genius seemed to guide
O'er Egypt's champaign, desolate and wide;
But here delightful beauty reigns alone,
And decks the morning scene with graces all her own.

KESWICK.—SIR GEORGE BEAUMONT

How shall I praise thee, Beaumont, whose nice skill
Can mould the soft and shadowy scene at will;
Chastise to harmony each gaudy ray,
Simple, yet grand, the mountain scene display;
The lake where sober evening seems to sleep,
Hills far retiring into umbrage deep;
Blend all with classic, pure, poetic taste,
And strike the more with forms and colours chaste!

MARKET-DAY.—CALCOT

Through the wood's maze our eyes delighted stray,
To mark the rustics on the market-day.
Beneath the branches winds the long white road;
Here peeps the rustic cottager's abode;
There in the morning sun, the children play,
Or the crone creeps along the dusty way.

SCENE IN FRANCE.—LOUTHERBOURG

Artist, I own thy genius; but the touch
May be too restless, and the glare too much:
And sure none ever saw a landscape shine,
Basking in beams of such a sun as thine,
But felt a fervid dew upon his phiz,
And panting cried, O Lord, how hot it is!

DEATH OF NELSON.—WEST

Turn to Britannia's triumphs on the main:
See Nelson, pale and fainting, 'mid the slain,
Whilst Victory sighs, stern in the garb of war,
And points through clouds the rocks of Trafalgar!
Here cease the strain; but while thy hulls shall ride,
Britain, dark shadowing the tumultuous tide,
May other Nelsons, on the sanguine main,
Guide, like a god, the battle's hurricane;
And when the funeral's transient pomp is past,
High hung the banner, hushed the battle's blast,
May the brave character to ages shine,
And Genius consecrate the immortal shrine!

SOUTHAMPTON CASTLE

INSCRIBED TO THE MARQUIS OF LANSDOWNE

The moonlight is without; and I could lose
An hour to gaze, though Taste and Splendour here,
As in a lustrous fairy palace, reign!
Regardless of the lights that blaze within,
I look upon the wide and silent sea,
That in the shadowy moonbeam sleeps:
How still,
Nor heard to murmur, or to move, it lies;
Shining in Fancy's eye, like the soft gleam,
The eve of pleasant yesterdays!
The clouds

Have all sunk westward, and the host of stars
Seem in their watches set, as gazing on;
While night's fair empress, sole and beautiful,
Holds her illustrious course through the mid heavens
Supreme, the spectacle, for such she looks,
Of gazing worlds!
How different is the scene
That lies beneath this arched window's height!
The town, that murmured through the busy day,
Is hushed; the roofs one solemn breadth of shade
Veils; but the towers, and taper spires above,
The pinnets, and the gray embattled walls,
And masts that throng around the southern pier,
Shine all distinct in light; and mark, remote,
O'er yonder elms, St Mary's modest fane.
Oh! if such views may please, to me they shine
How more attractive! but few years have passed,
Since there I saw youth, health, and happiness,
All circling round an aged sire, whose hairs
Are now in peace gone down; he was to me
A friend, and almost with a father's smile
Hung o'er my infant Muse. The cheerful voice
Of fellowship, the song of harmony,
And mirth, and wit, were there.
That scene is passed:
Cold death and separation have dissolved
The evening circle of once-happy friends!
So has it ever fared, and so must be,
With all! I see the moonlight watery tract
That shines far off, beneath the forest-shades:
What seems it, but the mirror of that tide,
Which noiseless, 'mid the changes of the world,
Holds its inevitable course, the tide
Of years departing; to the distant eye
Still seeming motionless, though hurrying on
From morn till midnight, bearing, as it flows,
The sails of pleasurable barks! These gleam
To-day, to-morrow other passing sails
Catch the like sunshine of the vernal morn.
Our pleasant days are as the moon's brief light
On the pale ripple, passing as it shines!
But shall the pensive bard for this lament,
Who knows how transitory are all worlds
Before His eye who made them!
Cease the strain;
And welcome still the social intercourse
That soothes the world's loud jarring, till the hour
When, universal darkness wrapping all

This nether scene, a light from heaven shall stream
Through clouds dividing, and a voice be heard:
Here only pure and lasting bliss is found!

THE WINDS

When dark November bade the leaves adieu,
And the gale sung amid the sea-boy's shrouds,
Methought I saw four winged forms, that flew,
With garments streaming light, amid the clouds;
From adverse regions of the sky,
In dim succession, they went by.
The first, as o'er the billowy deep he passed,
Blew from its brazen trump a far-resounding blast.
Upon a beaked promontory high,
With streaming heart, and cloudy brow severe,
Marked ye the father of the frowning year!
Dark vapours rolled o'er the tempestuous sky,
When creeping WINTER from his cave came forth;
Stern courier of the storm, he cried, what from the north?

NORTH WIND

From the vast and desert deeps,
Where the lonely Kraken sleeps,
Where fixed the icy mountains high
Glimmer to the twilight sky;
Where, six lingering months to last,
The night has closed, the day is past,
Father, lo, I come, I come:
I have heard the wizard's drum,
And the withered Lapland hag,
Seal, with muttered spell, her bag:
O'er mountains white, and forests sere,
I flew, and with a wink am here.

WINTER

Spirit of unwearied wing,
From the Baltic's frozen main,
From the Russ's bleak domain,
Say, what tidings dost thou bring!
Shouts, and the noise of battle! and again
The winged wind blew loud a deadly blast;

Shouts, and the noise of battle! the long main
Seemed with hoarse voice to answer as he passed.
The moody South went by, and silence kept;
The cloudy rack oft hid his mournful mien,
And frequent fell the showers, as if he wept
The eternal havoc of this mortal scene.
He had heard the yell, and cry,
And howling dance of Anarchy,
Where the Rhone, with rushing flood,
Murmured to the main, through blood:—
He seemed to wish he could for ever throw
His misty mantle o'er a world of woe.
But rousing him from his desponding trance,
Cold Eurus blew his sharp and shrilling horn;
In his right hand he bore an icy lance,
That far off glittered in the frost of morn;
The old man knew the clarion from afar,
What from the East? he cried.

EAST WIND

Shouts, and the noise of war!
Far o'er the land hath been my flight,
O'er many a forest dark as night,
O'er champaigns where the Tartar speeds,
O'er Wolga's wild and giant reeds,
O'er the Carpathian summits hoar,
Beneath whose snows and shadows frore,
Poland's level length unfolds
Her trackless woods and wildering wolds,
Like a spirit, seeking rest,
I have passed from east to west,
While sounds of discord and lament
Rose from the earth where'er I went.
I care not; hurrying, as in scorn,
I shook my lance, and blew my horn;
The day shows clear; and merrily
Along the Atlantic now I fly.
Who comes in soft and spicy vest,
From the mild regions of the West?
An azure veil bends waving o'er his head,
And showers of violets from his hands are shed.
'Tis Zephyr, with a look as young and fair
As when his lucid wings conveyed
That beautiful and gentle maid
Psyche, transported through the air,
The blissful couch of Love's own god to share.

Winter, avaunt! thy haggard eye
Will scare him, as he wanders by,
Him and the timid butterfly.
He brings again the morn of May;
The lark, amid the clear blue sky,
Carols, but is not seen so high,
And all the winter's winds fly far away!
I cried: O Father of the world, whose might
The storm, the darkness, and the winds obey,
Oh, when will thus the long tempestuous night
Of warfare and of woe be rolled away!
Oh, when will cease the uproar and the din,
And Peace breathe soft, Summer is coming in!

ON WILLIAM SOMMERS OF BREMHILL

When will the grave shelter thy few gray hairs,
O aged man! Thy sand is almost run,
And many a year, in vain, to meet the sun,
Thine eyes have rolled in darkness; want and cares
Have been thy visitants from morn to morn.
While trembling on existence thou dost live,
Accept what human charity can give;
But standing thus, time-palsied, and forlorn,
Like a scathed oak, of all its boughs bereft,
God and the grave are thy best refuge left.
When the bells rung, and summer's smiling ray
Welcomed again the merry Whitsuntide,
And all my humble villagers were gay;
I saw thee sitting on the highway side,
To feel once more the warm sun's blessed beam:
Didst thou then think upon thy own gay prime,
On such a holiday, and the glad time
When thou wert young and happy, like a dream
Now perished! No; the murmured prayer alone
Rose from the trembling lips towards the Throne
Of Mercy; that ere spring returned again,
And the long winter blew its dreary blast,
To sweep the verdure from the fading plain,
Thy burden would be dropped, thy sorrows past!
O blind and aged man, bowed down with cares,
When will the grave shelter thy few gray hairs!

THE VISIONARY BOY

Oh! lend that lute, sweet Archimage, to me!
Enough of care and heaviness
The weary lids of life depress,
And doubly blest that gentle heart shall be,
That wooes of poesy the visions bland,
And strays forgetful o'er enchanted land!
Oh! lend that lute, sweet Archimage, to me!
So spoke, with ardent look, yet eyebrow sad,
When he had passed o'er many a mountain rude,
And many a wild and weary solitude,
'Mid a green vale, a wandering minstrel-lad.
With eyes that shone in softened flame,
With wings and wand, young Fancy came;
And as she touched a trembling lute,
The lone enthusiast stood entranced and mute.
It was a sound that made his soul forego
All thoughts of sadness in a world of woe.
Oh, lend that lute! he cried: Hope, Pity, Love,
Shall listen; and each valley, rock, and grove,
Shall witness, as with deep delight,
From orient morn to dewy-stealing night.
My spirit, rapt in trance of sweetness high,
Shall drink the heartfelt sound with tears of ecstasy!
As thus he spoke, soft voices seemed to say,
Come away, come away;
Where shall the heart-sick minstrel stray,
But (viewing all things like a dream)
By haunted wood, or wizard stream?
That, like a hermit weeping,
Amid the gray stones creeping;
With voice distinct, yet faint,
Calls on Repose herself to hear its soothing plaint.
For him, romantic Solitude
Shall pile sublime her mountains rude;
For him, with shades more soft impressed,
The lucid lake's transparent breast
Shall show the banks, the woods, the hill,
More clear, more beautiful, more still.
For him more musical shall wave
The pines o'er Echo's moonlit cave;
While sounds as of a fairy lyre
Amid the shadowy cliffs expire!
This valley where the raptured minstrel stood
Was shaded with a circling slope of wood,
And rich in beauty, with that valley vied,
Thessalian Tempe, crowned with verdant bay,
Where smooth and clear Peneus winds his way;
And Ossa and Olympus, on each side,

Rise dark with woods; or that Sicilian plain
Which Arethusa's clearest waters lave,
By many a haunt of Pan, and wood-nymph's cave,
Lingering and listening to the Doric strain
Of him, the bard whose music might succeed
To the wild melodies of Pan's own reed!
This scene the mistress of the valley held,
Fancy, a magic maid; and at her will,
Aërial castles crowned the gleaming hill,
Or forests rose, or lapse of water welled.
Sometimes she sat with lifted eye,
And marked the dark storm in the western sky;
Sometimes she looked, and scarce her breath would draw,
As fearful things, not to be told, she saw;
And sometimes, like a vision of the air,
On wings of shifting light she floated here and there.
In the breeze her garments flew,
Of the brightest skiey blue,
Lucid as the tints of morn,
When Summer trills his pipe of corn:
Her tresses to each wing descending fall,
Or, lifted by the wind,
Stream loose and unconfined,
Like golden threads, beneath her myrtle coronal.
The listening passions stood aloof and mute,
As oft the west wind touched her trembling lute.
But when its sounds the youthful minstrel heard,
Strange mingled feelings, not to be expressed,
Rose undefined, yet blissful, on his breast,
And all the softened scene in sweeter light appeared.
Then Fancy waved her wand, and lo!
An airy troop went beckoning by:
Come, from toil and worldly woe;
Come, live with us in vales remote! they cry.
These are the flitting phantasies; the dreams
That lead the heart through all that elfin land,
Where half-seen shapes entice with whispers bland.
Meantime the clouds, impressed with livelier beams,
Roll, in the lucid track of air,
Arrayed in coloured brede, with semblances more fair.
The airy troop, as on they sail,
Thus the pensive stranger hail:
In the pure and argent sky,
There our distant chambers lie;
The bed is strewed with blushing roses,
When Quietude at eve reposes,
Oft trembling lest her bowers should fade,
In the cold earth's humid shade.

Come, rest with us! evanishing, they cried—
Come, rest with us! the lonely vale replied.
Then Fancy beckoned, and with smiling mien,
A radiant form arose, like the fair Queen
Of Beauty: from her eye divinely bright,
A richer lustre shot, a more attractive light.
She said: With fairer tints I can adorn
The living landscape, fairer than the morn.
The summer clouds in shapes romantic rolled,
And those they edge the fading west, like gold;
The lake that sleeps in sunlight, yet impressed
With shades more sweet than real on its breast;
'Mid baffling stones, beneath a partial ray,
The small brook huddling its uneven way;
The blue far distant hills, the silvery sea,
And every scene of summer speaks of me:
But most I wake the sweetest wishes warm,
Where the fond gaze is turned on woman's breathing form.
So passing silent through a myrtle grove,
Beauty first led him to the bower of Love.
A mellow light through the dim covert strayed,
And opening roses canopied the shade.
Why does the hurrying pulse unbidden leap!
Behold, in yonder glade that nymph asleep!
The heart-struck minstrel hangs, with lingering gaze,
O'er every charm his eye impassioned strays!
An edge of white is seen, and scarcely seen,
As soft she breathes, her coral lips between;
A lambent ray steals from her half-closed eye,
As her breast heaves a short imperfect sigh.
Sleep, winds of summer, o'er the leafy bower,
Nor move the light bells of the nodding flower;
Lest but a sound of stirring leaves might seem
To break the charm of her delicious dream!
And ye, fond, rising, throbbing thoughts, away,
Lest syren Pleasure all the soul betray!
Oh! turn, and listen to the ditty
From the lowly cave of Pity.
On slaughter's plain, while Valour grieves,
There he sunk to rest,
And the ring-dove scattered leaves
Upon his bleeding breast!
Her face was hid, while her pale arms enfold
What seemed an urn of alabaster cold;
To this she pressed her heaving bosom bare:
The drops that gathered in the dank abode
Fell dripping, on her long dishevelled hair;
And still her tears, renewed, and silent, flowed:

And when the winds of autumn ceased to swell,
At times was heard a slow and melancholy knell!
'Twas in the twilight of the deepest wood,
Beneath whose boughs like sad Cocytus, famed
Through fabling Greece, from lamentation named
A river dark and silent flowed, there stood
A pale and melancholy man, intent
His look upon that drowsy stream he bent,
As ever counting, when the fitful breeze
With strange and hollow sound sung through the trees,
Counting the sallow leaves, that down the current went.
He saw them not:
Earth seemed to him one universal blot.
Sometimes, as most distempered, to and fro
He paced; and sometimes fixed his chilling look
Upon a dreadful book,
Inscribed with secret characters of woe;
While gibbering imps, as mocking him, appeared,
And airy laughter 'mid the dusk was heard.
Then Fancy waved her wand again,
And all that valley that so lovely smiled
Was changed to a bare champaign, waste and wild.
"What pale and phantom-horseman rides amain?"
'Tis Terror;—all the plain, far on, is spread
With skulls and bones, and relics of the dead!
From his black trump he blew a louder blast,
And earthquakes muttered as the giant passed.
Then said that magic maid, with aspect bland,
'Tis thine to seize his phantom spear,
'Tis thine his sable trumpet to command,
And thrill the inmost heart with shuddering fear.
But hark! to Music's softer sound,
New scenes and fairer views accordant rise:
Above, around,
The mingled measure swells in air, and dies.
Music, in thy charmed shell,
What sounds of holy magic dwell!
Oft when that shell was to the ear applied,
Confusion of rich harmonies,
All swelling rose,
That came, as with a gently-swelling tide:
Then at the close,
Angelic voices seemed, aloft,
To answer as it died the cadence soft.
Now, like the hum of distant ocean's stream,
The murmurs of the wond'rous concave seem;
And now exultingly their tones prolong
The chorded pæans of the choral song,

Then Music, with a voice more wildly sweet
Than winds that pipe on the forsaken shore,
When the last rain-drops of the west are o'er,
Warbled: Oh, welcome to my blest retreat,
And give my sounds to the responsive lyre:
With me to these melodious groves retire,
And such pure feelings share,
As, far from noise and folly, soothe thee there.
Here Fancy, as the prize were won,
And now she hailed her favourite son,
With energy impatient cried:
The weary world is dark and wide,
Lo! I am with thee still to comfort and to guide.
Nor fear, if, grim before thine eyes,
Pale worldly Want, a spectre, lowers;
What is a world of vanities
To a world as sweet as ours!
When thy heart is sad and lone,
And loves to dwell on pleasures flown,
When that heart no more shall bound
At some kind voice's well-known sound,
My spells thy drooping languor shall relieve,
And airy spirits touch thy lonely harp at eve.
Look!—Delight and Hope advancing,
Music joins her thrilling notes,
O'er the level lea come dancing;
Seize the vision as it floats,
Bright-eyed Rapture hovers o'er them,
Waving light his seraph wings,
Youth exulting flies before them,
Scattering cowslips as he sings!
Come now, my car pursue,
The wayward Fairy cried;
And high amid the fields of air,
Above the clouds, together we will ride,
And posting on the viewless winds,
So leave the cares of earth and all its thoughts behind.
I can sail, and I can fly,
To all regions of the sky,
On the shooting meteor's course,
On a winged griffin-horse!
She spoke: when Wisdom's self drew nigh,
A noble sternness in her searching eye;
Like Pallas helmed, and in her hand a spear,
As not in idle warfare bent, but still,
As resolute, to cope with every earthly ill.
In youthful dignity severe,
She stood: And shall the aspiring mind,

To Fancy be alone resigned!
Alas! she cried, her witching lay
Too often leads the heart astray!
Still, weak minstrel, wouldst thou rove,
Drooping in the distant grove,
Forgetful of all ties that bind
Thee, a brother, to mankind?
Has Fancy's feeble voice defied
The ills to poor humanity allied?
Can she, like Wisdom, bid thy soul sustain
Its post of duty in a life of pain!
Can she, like meek Religion, bid thee bear
Contempt and hardship in a world of care!
Yet let not my rebuke decry,
In all, her blameless witchery,
Or from the languid bosom tear
Each sweet illusion nourished there.
With dignity and truth, combined,
Still may she rule the manly mind;
Her sweetest magic still impart
To soften, not subdue, the heart:
Still may she warm the chosen breast,
Not as the sovereign, but the guest.
Then shall she lead the blameless Muse
Through all her fairest, wildest views;
To mark amid the flowers of morn,
The bee go forth with early horn;
Or when the moon, a softer light
Sheds on the rocks and seas of night,
To hear the circling fairy bands
Sing, Come unto these yellow sands!
Sweeter is our light than day,
Fond enthusiast, come away!
Then Chivalry again shall call
The champions to her bannered hall!
The pipe, and song, with many a mingled shout,
Ring through the forest, as the satyr-rout,
Dance round the dragon-chariot of Romance;
Forth pricks the errant knight with rested lance;
Imps, demons, fays, in antic train succeed,
The wandering maiden, and the winged steed!
The muttering wizard turns, with haggard look,
The bloody leaves of the accursed book,
Whilst giants, from the gloomy castle tower,
With lifted bats of steel, more dreadful lower!
At times, the magic shall prevail
Of the wild and wonderous tale;
At times, high rapture shall prolong

The deep, enthusiastic song.
Hence, at midnight, thou shalt stray,
Where dark ocean flings its spray,
To hear o'er heaven's resounding arch
The Thunder-Lord begin his march!
Or mark the flashes, that present
Some far-off shattered monument;
Whilst along the rocky vale,
Red fires, mingled with the hail,
Run along upon the ground,
And the thunders deeper sound!
The loftier Muse, with awful mien,
Upon a lonely rock is seen:
Full is the eye that speaks the dauntless soul;
She seems to hear the gathering tempest roll
Beneath her feet; she bids an eagle fly,
Breasting the whirlwind, through the dark-red sky;
Or, with elated look, lifts high the spear,
As sounds of distant battles roll more near.
Now deep-hushed in holy trance,
She sees the powers of Heaven advance,
And wheels, instinct with spirit, bear
God's living chariot through the air;
Now on the wings of morn she seems to rise,
And join the strain of more than mortal harmonies.
Thy heart shall beat exulting as she sings,
And thou shalt cry: Give me an angel's wings!
With sadder sound, o'er Pity's cave,
The willow in the wind shall wave;
And all the listening passions stand,
Obedient to thy great command.
With Poesy's sweet charm impressed,
Fancy thus shall warm thy breast;
Still her smiling train be thine,
Still her lovely visions shine,
To cheer, beyond my boasted power,
A sad or solitary hour.
Thus let them soothe a while thy heart,
"Come like shadows, so depart;"
But never may the witching lay
Lead each sense from life astray;
For vain the poet's muse of fire,
Vain the magic of his lyre,
Unless the touch subdued impart
Truth and wisdom to the heart!

CADLAND, SOUTHAMPTON RIVER

If ever sea-maid, from her coral cave,
Beneath the hum of the great surge, has loved
To pass delighted from her green abode,
And, seated on a summer bank, to sing
No earthly music; in a spot like this,
The bard might feign he heard her, as she dried
Her golden hair, yet dripping from the main,
In the slant sunbeam.

So the pensive bard
Might image, warmed by this enchanting scene,
The ideal form; but though such things are not,
He who has ever felt a thought refined;
He who has wandered on the sea of life,
Forming delightful visions of a home
Of beauty and repose; he who has loved,
With filial warmth his country, will not pass
Without a look of more than tenderness
On all the scene; from where the pensile birch
Bends on the bank, amid the clustered group
Of the dark hollies; to the woody shore
That steals diminished, to the distant spires
Of Hampton, crowning the long lucid wave.
White in the sun, beneath the forest-shade,
Full shines the frequent sail, like Vanity,
As she goes onward in her glittering trim,
Amid the glances of life's transient morn,
Calling on all to view her!

Vectis there,
That slopes its greensward to the lambent wave,
And shows through softest haze its woods and domes,
With gray St Catherine's creeping to the sky,
Seems like a modest maid, who charms the more
Concealing half her beauties.

To the East,
Proud, yet complacent, on its subject realm,
With masts innumerable thronged, and hulls
Seen indistinct, but formidable, mark
Albion's vast fleet, that, like the impatient storm,
Waits but the word to thunder and flash death
On him who dares approach to violate
The shores and living scenes that smile secure
Beneath its dragon-watch!
Long may they smile!

And long, majestic Albion (while the sound
From East to West, from Albis to the Po,
Of dark contention hurtles), may'st thou rest,
As calm and beautiful this sylvan scene
Looks on the refluent wave that steals below.

THE LAST SONG OF CAMOENS

The morning shone on Tagus' rocky side,
And airs of summer swelled the yellow tide,
When, rising from his melancholy bed,
And faint, and feebly by Antonio led,
Poor Camoens, subdued by want and woe,
Along the winding margin wandered slow,
His harp, that once could each warm feeling move
Of patriot glory or of tenderest love,
His sole and sable friend (while a faint tone
Rose from the wires) placed by a mossy stone.
How beautiful the sun ascending shines
From ridge to ridge, along the purple vines!
How pure the azure of the opening skies!
How resonant the nearer rock replies
To call of early mariners! and, hark!
The distant whistle from yon parting bark,
That down the channel as serene she strays,
Her gray sail mingles with the morning haze,
Bound to explore, o'er ocean's stormy reign,
New lands that lurk amid the lonely main!
A transient fervour touched the old man's breast;
He raised his eyes, so long by care depressed,
And while they shone with momentary fire,
Ardent he struck the long-forgotten lyre.
From Tagus' yellow-sanded shore,
O'er the billows, as they roar,
O'er the blue sea, waste and wide,
Our bark threw back the burning tide,
By northern breezes cheer'ly borne,
On to the kingdoms of the morn.
Blanco, whose cold shadow vast
Chills the western wave, is past!
Huge Bojador, frowning high,
Thy dismal terrors we defy!
But who may violate the sleep
And silence of the sultry deep;
Where, beneath the intenser sun,
Hot showers descend, red lightnings run;

Whilst all the pale expanse beneath
Lies burning wide, without a breath;
And at mid-day from the mast,
No shadow on the deck is cast!
Night by night, still seen the same,
Strange lights along the cordage flame,
Perhaps, the spirits of the good,
That wander this forsaken flood
Sing to the seas, as slow we float,
A solemn and a holy note!
Spectre of the southern main,
Thou barr'st our onward way in vain,
Wrapping the terrors of thy form,
In the thunder's rolling storm!
Fearless o'er the indignant tide,
On to the east our galleys ride.
Triumph! for the toil is o'er—
We kiss the far-sought Indian shore!
Glittering to the orient ray,
The banners of the Cross display!
Does my heart exulting bound?
Alas, forlorn, I gaze around:
Feeble, poor, and old, I stand,
A stranger in my native land!
My sable slave (ah, no! my only friend,
Whose steps upon my rugged path attend)
Sees, but with tenderness that fears to speak,
The tear that trickles down my aged cheek!
My harp is silent,—famine shrinks mine eye,—
"Give me a little food for charity!"

Camoens, the great poet of Portugal, is supposed to have gone to the East Indies in the same ship with the first Discoverer, round the Cape of Good Hope, Vasco de Gama. This is not the case, though he wrote the noble poem descriptive of the voyage. He went to India some years afterwards, but the general idea is sufficient for poetical purposes. His subsequent sorrows and poverty, in his native land, are well known.

THE SYLPH OF SUMMER

God said, Let there be light, and there was light!
At once the glorious sun, at his command,
From space illimitable, void and dark,
Sprang jubilant, and angel hierarchies,
Whose long hosannahs pealed from orb to orb,
Sang, Glory be to Thee, God of all worlds!
Then beautiful the ball of this terrene

Rolled in the beam of first-created day,
And all its elements obeyed the voice
Of Him, the great Creator; Air, and Fire,
And Earth, and Water, each its ministry
Performed, whilst Chaos from his ebon throne
Leaped up; and so magnificent, and decked,
And mantled in its ambient atmosphere,
The living world began its state!

To thee,
Spirit of Air, I lift the venturous song,
Whose viewless presence fills the living scene,
Whose element ten thousand thousand wings
Fan joyous; o'er whose fields the morning clouds
Ride high; whose rule the lightning-shafts obey,
And the deep thunder's long-careering march!
The Winds too are thy subjects; from the breeze,
That, like a child upon a holiday,
On the high mountain's van pursues the down
Of the gray thistle, ere the autumnal shower
Steals soft, and mars his pastime; to the King
Of Hurricanes, that sounds his mighty shell,
And bids Tornado sweep the Western world.
Sylph of the Summer Gale, on thee I call!
Oh, come, when now gay June is in her car,
Wafting the breath of roses as she moves;
Come to this garden bower, which I have hung
With tendrils, and the fragrant eglantine,
And mandrake, rich with many mantling stars!
'Tis pleasant, when thy breath is on the leaves
Without, to rest in this embowering shade,
And mark the green fly, circling to and fro,
O'er the still water, with his dragon wings,
Shooting from bank to bank, now in quick turns,
Then swift athwart, as is the gazer's glance,
Pursuing still his mate; they, with delight,
As if they moved in morris, to the sound
Harmonious of this ever-dripping rill,
Now in advance, now in retreat, now round,
Dart through their mazy rings, and seem to say:
The Summer and the Sun are ours!

But thou,
Sylph of the Summer Gale, delay a while
Thy airy flight, whilst here Francesca leans,
And, charmed by Ossian's harp, seems in the breeze
To hear Malvina's plaint; thou to her ear
Come unperceived, like music of the song

From Cona's vale of streams; then with the bee,
That sounds his horn, busied from flower to flower,
Speed o'er the yellow meadows, breathing ripe
Their summer incense; or amid the furze,
That paints with bloom intense the upland crofts,
With momentary essence tinge thy wings;
Or in the grassy lanes, one after one,
Lift light the nodding foxglove's purple bell.
Thence, to the distant sea, and where the flag
Hangs idly down, without a wavy curl,
Thou hoverest o'er the topmast, or dost raise
The full and flowing mainsail: Steadily,
The helmsman cries, as now thy breath is heard
Among the stirring cordage o'er his head;
So, steadily, he cries, as right he steers,
Speeds our proud ship along the world of waves.
Sylph, may thy favouring breath more gently blow,
More gently round the temples and the cheek
Of him, who, leaving home and friends behind,
In silence musing o'er the ocean leans,
And watches every passing shade that marks
The southern Channel's fast-retiring line;
Then, as the ship rolls on, keeps a long look
Fixed on the lessening Lizard, the last point
Of that delightful country, where he left
All his fond hopes behind: it lessens still;
Still, still it lessens, and now disappears!
He turns, and only sees the waves that rock
Boundless. How many anxious morns shall rise,
How many moons shall light the farthest seas,
O'er what new scenes and regions shall he stray,
A weary man, still thinking of his home,
Ere he again that shore shall view, and greet
With blissful thronging hopes and starting tears,
Of heartfelt welcome, and of warmest love!
Perhaps, ah! never! So didst thou go forth,
My poor lost brother!
The airs of morning as enticing played,
And gently, round thee, and their whisperings
Might sooth (if aught could sooth) a boding heart;
For thou wert bound to visit scenes of death,
Where the sick gale (alas! unlike the breeze
That bore the gently-swelling sail along)
Was tainted with the breath of pestilence,
That smote the silent camp, and night and day
Sat mocking on the putrid carcases.
Thou too didst perish! As the south-west blows,
Thy bones, perhaps, now whiten on the coast

Of old Algarva. I, meantime, these shades
Of village solitude, hoping erewhile
To welcome thee from many a toil restored,
Still deck, and now thy empty urn alone
I meet, where, swaying in the summer gale,
The willow whispers in my evening walk.
Sylph, in thy airy robe, I see thee float,
A rainbow o'er thy head, and in thy hand
The magic instrument, that, as thy wing,
Lucid, and painted like the butterfly's,
Waves to and from, most musically rings;
Sometimes in joyance, as the flaunting leaf
Of the white poplar, sometimes sad and slow,
As bearing pensive airs from Pity's grave.
Soft child of air, thou tendest on his sway,
As gentle Ariel at the bidding hies
Of mighty Prospero; yet other winds
Throng to his wizard 'hest, inspiring some,
Some melancholy, and yet soothing much
The drooping wanderer in the fading copse;
Some terrible, with solitude and death
Attendant on their march:—the wild Simoom,
Riding on whirling spires of burning sand,
That move along the Nubian wilderness,
And bury deep the silent caravan;—
Monsoon, up-starting from his half-year sleep,
Upon the vernal shores of Hindostan,
And tempesting with sounds of torrent rain,
And hail, the darkening main;—and red Sameel,
Blasting and withering, like a rivelled leaf,
The pilgrim as he roams;—Sirocco sad,
That pants, all summer, on the cloudless shores
Of faint Parthenope;—deep in the mine
Oft lurks the lurid messenger of death,
The ghastly fiend that blows, when the pale light
Quivers, and leaves the gasping wretch to die;—
The imp, that when the hollow curfew knolls,
Wanders the misty marish, lighting it
At night with errant and fantastic flame.
Spirit of air, these are thy ministers,
That wait thy will; but thou art all in all,
And dead without thee were the flower, the leaf,
The waving forest rivelled, the great sea
Still, the lithe birds of heaven extinct, and ceased
The soul of melting music.

This fair scene
Lives in thy tender touch, for so It seems;

Whilst universal nature owns thy sway;
From the mute insect on the summer pool,
That with long cobweb legs, firm as on earth
The ostrich skims, flits idly to and fro,
Making no dimple on the watery mass;
To the huge grampus, spouting, as he rolls,
A cataract, amid the cold clear sky,
And furrowing far and wide the northern deep.
Thy presence permeates and fills the whole!
As the poor butterfly, that, painted gay,
With mealy wings, red, amber, white, or dropped
With golden stains, floats o'er the yellow corn,
Idly, as bent on pastime, while the morn
Smiles on his devious voyage; if inclosed
In the exhausted prison, whence thy breath
With suction slow is drawn, he feels the change
How dire! in palsied inanition drops!
Weak flags his weary wing, and weaker yet;
His frame with tremulous convulsion moves
A moment, and the next is still in death.
So were the great and glorious world itself;
The tenants of its continents, all ceased!
A wide, a motionless, a putrid waste,
Its seas! How droops the languid mariner,
When not a breath, along the sluggish main,
Strays on the sultry surface as it sleeps;
When far away the winds are flown, to dash
The congregated ocean on the Cape
Of Southern Africa, leaving the while
The flood's vast surface noiseless, waveless, white,
Beneath Mozambique's long-reflected woods,
A gleaming mirror, spread from east to west,
Where the still ship, as on a bed of glass,
Sits motionless. Awake, ye hurricanes!
Ye winds that harrow up the wintry waste,
Awake! for Thunder in his sounding car,
Flashing thick lightning from the rolling wheels,
And the red volley, charged with instant death,
Were music to this lingering, sickening calm,
The same eternal sunshine; still, all still,
Without a vapour, or a sound.

If thus,
Beneath the burning, breathless atmosphere,
Faint Nature sickening droop; who shall ascend
The height, where Silence, since the world began,
Has sat on Cimborazzo's highest peak,
A thousand toises o'er the cloud's career,

Soaring in finest ether? Far below,
He sees the mountains burning at his feet,
Whose smoke ne'er reached his forehead; never there,
Though the black whirlwind shake the distant shores,
The passing gale has murmured; never there
The eagle's cry has echoed; never there
The solitary condor's weary wing
Hath yet ascended!

Let the rising thought
Beyond the confines of this vapoury vault
Be lifted, to the boundless void of space,
How dread, how infinite! where other worlds,
Ten million and ten million leagues aloft,
In other precincts with their shadows roll.
There roams the sole erratic comet, borne
With lightning speed, yet twice three hundred years
Its destined course accomplishing.

Then whirled,
Far from the attractive orb of central fire,
Back through the dim and infinite abyss,
Dread flaming visitant, ere thou return'st,
Empires may rise and fail; the palaces,
That shone on earth, may vanish like the dews
Of morning, scarce illumined ere they fly.
Dread flaming visitant, who that pursues
Thy long and lonely voyage, ev'n in thought,
(Till thought itself seem in the effort lost,)
But tremblingly exclaims, There is a God:
There is a God who lights ten thousand suns,
Round which revolve worlds wheeling amid worlds.
He launched thy voyage through the vast abyss,
He hears his universe, through all its orbs,
As with one voice, proclaim,
There is a God!

Lifted above this dim diurnal sphere,
So fancy, rising with her theme, ascends,
And voyaging the illimitable void,
Where comets flame, sees other worlds and suns
Emerge, and on this earth, like a dim speck,
Looks down: nor in the wonderful and vast
Of the dread scene magnificent, she views
Alone the Almighty Ruler, but the web
That shines in summer time, and only seen
In the slant sunbeam, wakes a moral thought.
In autumn, when the thin long spider gains

The leafy bush's top, he from his seat
Shoots the soft filament, like threads of air,
Scarce seen, into the sky; and thus sustained,
Boldly ascends into the breezy void,
Dependent on the trembling line he wove,
Insidious, and intent on scenes of spoil
And death:—So mounts Ambition, and aloft
On his proud summit meditates new scenes
Of plunder and dominion, till the breeze
Of fortune change, that blows to empty air
His feeble, frail support, and once again
Leaves him a reptile, struggling in the dust!
But what the world itself, what in His view
Whose dread Omnipotence is over all!
A twinkling air-thread in the vast of space.
And what the works of that proud insect, Man!
His mausoleums, fanes, and pyramids,
Frown in the dusk of long-revolving years,
While generations, as they rise and drop,
Each following each to silence and to dust,
Point as they pass, and say, It was a God
That made them: but nor date, nor name
Oblivion shows; cloud only, rolling on,
And wrapping darker as it rolls, the works
Of man!

Now raised on Contemplation's wing,
The blue vault, fervent with unnumbered stars,
He ranges: speeds, as with an angel's flight,
From orb to orb; sees distant suns illume
The boundless space, then bends his head to earth,
So poor is all he knows!

O'er sanguine fields
Now rides he, armed and crested like the god
Of fabled battles; where he points, pale Death
Strides over weltering carcases; nor leaves,—
But still a horrid shadow, step by step,
Stalks mocking after him, till now the noise
Of rolling acclamation, and the shout
Of multitude on multitude, is past:
The scene of all his triumphs, wormy earth,
Closes upon his perishable pride;
For "dust he is, and shall to dust return"!
But Conscience, a small voice from heaven replies,
Conscience shall meet him in another world.
Let man, then, walk meek, humble, pure, and just;
Though meek, yet dignified; though humble, raised,

The heir of life and immortality;
Conscious that in this awful world he stands,
He only of all living things, ordained
To think, and know, and feel, there is a God!
Child of the air, though most I love to hear
Thy gentle summons whisper, when the Spring,
At the first carol of the village lark,
Looks out and smiles, or June is in her car;
Not undelightful is the purer air
In winter, when the keen north-east is high,
When frost fantastic his cold garland weaves
Of brittle flowers, or soft-succeeding snows
Gather without apace, and heavy load
The berried sweetbrier, clinging to my pane.
The blackbird, then, that marks the ruddy pods
Peep through the snow, though silent is his song,
Yet, pressed by cold and hunger, ventures near.
The robin group, familiar, muster round
The garden-shed, where, at his dinner set,
The laboured hind strews here and there a crumb
From his brown bread; then heedless of the winds
That blow without, and sweep the shivered snow,
Sees from his broken tube the smoke ascend
On an inverted barrow, as in state
He sits, though poor, the monarch of the scene,
As pondering deep the garden's future state,
His kingdom; the rude instruments of death
Lie at his feet, fashioned with simple skill,
With which he hopes to snare the prowling race,
The mice, rapacious of his vernal hopes.
So seated, on the spring he ruminates,
And solemn as a sophi, moves nor hand,
Nor eye, till haply some more venturous bird,
(The crumbs exhausted that he lately strewed
Upon the groundsill,) with often dipping beak,
And sidelong look, as asking larger dole,
Comes hopping to his feet: and say, ye great,
Ye mighty monarchs of this earthly scene,
What nobler views can elevate the heart
Of a proud patriot king, than thus to chase
The bold rapacious spoilers from the field,
And with an eye of merciful regard
To look on humble worth, wet from the storm,
And chilled by indigence!

But thoughts like these
Ill suit the radiant summer's rosy prime,
And the still temper of the calm blue sky.

The sunny shower is past; at intervals
The silent glittering drops descend; and mark,
Upon the blue bank of yon western cloud,
That looms direct against the emerging orb,
How bright, how beautiful the rainbow's hues
Steal out, how stately bends the graceful arch
Above the hills, and tinging at his foot
The mead and trees! Fancy might think young Hope
Pants for the vision, and with ardent eye
Pursues the unreal shade, and spreads her hands,
Weeping to see it fade, as all her dreams
Have faded.

These, O Air! are but the toys,
That sometimes deck thy fairy element;
So oft the eye observant loves to trace
The colours, and the shadows, and the forms,
That wander o'er the veering atmosphere.
See, in the east, the rare parhelia shine
In mimic glory, and so seem to mock
(Fixed parallel to the ascending orb)
The majesty, the splendour, and the shape,
Of the sole luminary that informs
The world with light and heat! The halo-ring
Bends over all!

With desultory shafts,
And long and arrowy glance, the night-lights shoot
Pale coruscations o'er the northern sky;
Now lancing to the cope, in sheets of flame,
Now wavering wild, as the reflected wave,
On the arched roof of the umbrageous grot.
Hence Superstition dreams of armaments,
Of fiery conflicts, and of bleeding fields
Of slaughter; so on great Jerusalem,
Ere yet she fell, the flaming meteor glared;
A waving sword ensanguined seemed to point
To the devoted city, and a voice
Was heard, Depart, depart!

The atmosphere,
That with the ceaseless hurry of its clouds,
Encircles the round globe, resembles oft
The passing sunshine, or the glooms that stray
O'er every human spirit.

Thin light streaks
Of thought pass vapoury o'er the vacant mind,

And fade to nothing. Now fantastic gleams
Play, flashing or expiring, of gay hope,
Or deep despair; then clouds of sadness close
In one dark settled gloom, and all the man
Droops, in despondence lost.

Aërial tints
Please most the pensive poet: and the views
He forms, though evanescent, and as vain
As the air's mockery, seem to his eye
Ev'n as substantial images, and shapes,
Till in a hurrying rack they all dissolve.
So in the cloudless sky, amusive shines
The soft and mimic scenery; distant hills
That, in refracted light, hang beautiful
Beneath the golden car of eve, ere yet
The daylight lingering fades.

Hence, on the heights
Of Apennine, far stretching to the south,
The goat-herd, while the westering sun, far off,
Hangs o'er the hazy ocean's brim, beholds
In the horizon's faintly-glowing verge
A landscape, like the rainbow, rise, with rocks
That softened shine, and shores that trend away,
Beneath the winding woods of Sicily,
And Etna, smouldering in the still pale sky;
And dim Messina, with her spires, and bays
That wind among the mountains, and the tower
Of Faro, gleaming on the tranquil straits;
Unreal all, yet on the air impressed,
From light's refracted ray, the shadow seems
The certain scene: the hind astonished views,
Yet most delighted, till at once the light
Changes, and all has vanished!

But to him,
How different in still air the unreal view,
Who wanders in Arabian solitudes,
When, faint with thirst, he sees illusive streams
Shine in the arid desert!

All around,
A silent waste of dark gray sand is spread,
Like ashes; not a speck in heaven appears,
But the red sun, high in his burning noon,
Shoots down intolerable fire: no sound
Of beast, or blast, or moving insect, stirs

The horrid stillness. Oh! what hand will guide
The pilgrim, panting in the trackless dust,
To where the pure and sparkling fountain cheers
The green oasis. See, as now his lip
Hangs parched and quivering, see before him spread
The long and level lake!

He gazes; still
He gazes, till he drops upon the sands,
And to the vision stretches, as he faints,
His feeble hand.

Come, Sylph of Summer, come!
Return to these green pastures, that, remote
From fiery blasts, or deadly blistering frosts,
Beneath the temperate atmosphere rejoice!
A crown of flame, a javelin in his hand,
Like the red arrow that the lightning shoots
Through night, impetuous steeds, and burning wheels,
That, as they whirl, flash to the cope of heaven,
Proclaim the angel of the world of fire!
The ocean-king, lord of the waters, rides
High on his hissing car, whose concave skirrs
The azure deep beneath him, flashing wide,
As to the sun the dark-green wave upturns,
And foaming far behind: sea-horses breast
The bickering surge, with nostrils sounding far,
And eyes that flash above the wave, and necks,
Whose mane, like breakers whitening in the wind,
Toss through the broken foam: he kingly bears
His trident sceptre high; around him play
Nereids, and sea-maids, singing as he rides
Their choral song: huge Triton, weltering on,
With scaly train, at times his wreathed shell
Sounds, that the caverns of old ocean shake!
But milder thou, soft daughter of the air,
Sylph of the Summer, come! the silent shower
Is past, and 'mid the dripping fern, the wren
Peeps, till the sun looks through the clouds again.
Oh, come, and breathe thy gentler influence,
And send a home-felt quiet to my heart,
Soothed as I hear, by fits, thy whisper run,
Stirring the tall acacia's pendent leaves,
And through yon hazel alley rustling soft
Upon the vacant ear!

Yon eastern downs,
That weather-fence the blossoms of the vale,

Where winds from hill to hill the mighty Dike,
Of Woden named, with many an antique mound,
The warrior's grave, bids exercise awake,
And health, the breeze of morning to inhale:
Meantime, remote from storms, the myrtle blooms
Beneath my southern sash.

The hurricane
May rend the pines of snowy Labrador,
The blasting whirlwinds of the desert sweep
The Nubian wilderness—we fear them not;
Nor yet, my country, do thy breezes bear,
From citrons, or the blooming orange-grove,
As in Rousillon's jasmine-bordered vales,
Incense at eve.

But temperate airs are thine,
England; and as thy climate, so thy sons
Partake the temper of thine isle; not rude,
Nor soft, voluptuous, nor effeminate;
Sincere, indeed, and hardy, as becomes
Those who can lift their look elate, and say,
We strike for injured freedom; and yet mild,
And gentle, when the voice of charity
Pleads like a voice from heaven: and, thanks to GOD,
The chain that fettered Afric's groaning race,
The murderous chain, that, link by link, dropped blood,
Is severed; we have lost that foul reproach
To all our virtuous boast!

Humanity,
England, is thine! not that false substitute,
That meretricious sadness, which, all sighs
For lark or lambkin, yet can hear unmoved
The bloodiest orgies of blood-boltered France;
Thine is consistent, manly, rational,
Nor needing the false glow of sentiment
To melt it into sympathy, but mild,
And looking with a gentle eye on all;
Thy manners open, social, yet refined,
Are tempered with reflection; gaiety,
In her long-lighted halls, may lead the dance,
Or wake the sprightly chord; yet nature, truth,
Still warm the ingenuous heart: there is a blush
With those most gay, and lovely; and a tear
With those most manly!

Temperate Liberty

Hath yet the fairest altar on thy shores;
Such, and so warm with patriot energy,
As raised its arm when a false Stuart fled;
Yet mingled with deep wisdom's cautious lore,
That when it bade a Papal tyrant pause
And tremble, held the undeviating reins
On the fierce neck of headlong Anarchy.
Thy Church, (nor here let zealot bigotry,
Vaunting, condemn all altars but its own),
Thy Church, majestic, but not sumptuous,
Sober, but not austere, with lenity
Tempering her fair pre-eminence, sustains
Her liberal charities, yet decent state.
The tempest is abroad; the fearful sounds
Of armament, and gathering tumult, fill
The ear of anxious Europe. If, O GOD!
It is thy will, that in the storm of death,
When we have lifted the brave sword in vain,
We too should sink, sustain us in that hour!
Meantime be mine, in cheerful privacy,
To wait Thy will, not sanguine, nor depressed;
In even course, nor splendid, nor obscure,
To steal through life among my villagers!
The hum of the discordant crowd, the buzz
Of faction, the poor fly that threads the air
Self-pleased, the wasp that points its tiny sting
Unfelt, pass by me like the idle wind
That I regard not; while the Summer Sylph,
That whispers through the laurels, wakes the thought
Of quietude, and home-felt happiness,
And independence, in a land I love!

THE HARP OF HOEL

It was a high and holy sight,
When Baldwin and his train,
With cross and crosier gleaming bright,
Came chanting slow the solemn rite,
To Gwentland's pleasant plain.

High waved before, in crimson pride,
The banner of the Cross;
The silver rood was then descried,
While deacon youths, from side to side,
The fuming censer toss.

The monks went two and two along,
And winding through the glade,
Sang, as they passed, a holy song,
And harps and citterns, 'mid the throng,
A mingled music made.

They ceased; when lifting high his hand,
The white-robed prelate cried:
Arise, arise, at Christ's command,
To fight for his name in the Holy Land,
Where a Saviour lived and died!

With gloves of steel, and good broadsword,
And plumed helm of brass,
Hoel, Landoga's youthful lord,
To hear the father's holy word,
Came riding to the pass.

More earnestly the prelate spake:
Oh, heed no earthly loss!
He who will friends and home forsake,
Now let him kneel, and fearless take
The sign of the Holy Cross.

Then many a maid her tresses rent,
And did her love implore:
Oh, go not thou to banishment!
For me, and the pleasant vales of Gwent,
Thou never wilt see more.

And many a mother, pale with fears,
Did kiss her infant son;
Said, Who will shield thy helpless years,
Who dry thy widowed mother's tears,
When thy brave father's gone?

GOD, with firm voice the prelate cried,
God will the orphan bless;
Sustain the widow's heart, and guide
Through the hard world, obscure and wild,
The poor and fatherless.

Then might you see a shade o'ercast
Brave Hoel's ruddy hue,
But soon the moment's thought is past:—
Hark, hark, 'tis the trumpet's stirring blast!
And he grasped his bow of yew.

Then might you see a moment's gloom
Sit in brave Hoel's eye:
Make in the stranger's land my tomb,
I follow thee, be it my doom,
O CHRIST, to live or die!

No more he thought, though rich in fee,
Of any earthly loss,
But lighting, on his bended knee,
Said, Father, here I take from thee
The sign of the Holy Cross.

I have a wife, to me more dear
Then is my own heart's blood;
I have a child, (a starting tear,
Which soon he dried, of love sincere,
On his stern eyelid stood);

To them farewell! O God above,
Thine is the fate of war;
But oh! reward Gwenlhian's love,
And may my son a comfort prove,
When I am distant far!

Farewell, my harp!—away, away!
To the field of death I go;
Welcome the trumpet's blast, the neigh
Of my bold and barbed steed of gray,
And the clang of the steel crossbow!

Gwenlhian sat in the hall at night,
Counting the heavy hours;
She saw the moon, with tranquil light,
Shine on the circling mountain's height,
And the dim castle towers.

Deep stillness was on hill and glen,
When she heard a bugle blow;
A trump from the watch-tower answered then,
And the tramp of steeds, and the voice of men,
Were heard in the court below.

The watch-dog started at the noise,
Then crouched at his master's feet;
He knew his step, he heard his voice;
But who can now like her rejoice,
Who flies her own lord to greet?

And soon her arms his neck enfold:
But whence that altered mien!
O say, then, is thy love grown cold,
Or hast thou been hurt by the robbers bold,
That won in the forest of Dean?

Oh no, he cried, the God above,
Who all my soul can see,
Knows my sincere, my fervent love;
If aught my stern resolve could move,
It were one tear from thee.

But I have sworn, in the Holy Land,—
Need I the sequel speak;
Too well, she cried, I understand!
Then grasped in agony his hand,
And hid her face on his cheek.

My loved Gwenlhian, weep not so,
From the lid that tear I kiss;
Though to the wars far off I go,
Betide me weal, betide me woe,
We yet may meet in bliss.

Fourteen suns their course had rolled,
When firmly thus he spake;
Hear now my last request: behold
This ring, it is of purest gold,
Love, keep it for my sake!

When summers seven have robed each tree,
And clothed the vales with green,
If I come not back, then thou art free,
To wed or not, and to think of me,
As I had never been!

Nay, answer not,—what wouldst thou say!
Come, let my harp be brought;
For the last time, I fain would play,
Ere yet we part, our favourite lay,
And cheat severer thought:

Oh, cast every care to the wind,
And dry, best beloved, the tear!
Secure, that thou ever shalt find,
The friend of thy bosom sincere.
Still friendship shall live in the breast of the brave,
And we'll love, the long day, where the forest-trees wave.

I have felt each emotion of bliss,
That affection the fondest can prove,
Have received on my lip the first kiss
Of thy holy and innocent love;
But perish each hope of delight,
Like the flashes of night on the sea,
If ever, though far from thy sight,
My soul is forgetful of thee!
Still the memory shall live in the breast of the brave,
How we loved, the long day, where the forest-trees wave.

Now bring my boy; may God above
Shower blessings on his head!
May he requite his mother's love,
And to her age a comfort prove,
When I perhaps am dead!

The beams of morn on his helm did play,
And aloud the bugle blew,
Then he leaped on his harnessed steed of gray,
And sighed to the winds as he gallopedf away,
Adieu, my heart's love, adieu!

And now he has joined the warrior train
Of knights and barons bold,
That, bound to Salem's holy plain,
Across the gently-swelling main,
Their course exulting hold.

With a cross of gold, as on they passed,
The crimson streamers flew;
The shields hung glittering round the mast,
And on the waves a radiance cast,
Whilst all the trumpets blew.

O'er the Severn-surge, in long array,
So, the proud galleys went,
Till soon, as dissolved in ether gray,
The woods, and the shores, and the Holms steal away,
And the long blue hills of Gwent.

PART II

High on the hill, with moss o'ergrown,
A hermit chapel stood;

It spoke the tale of seasons gone,
And half-revealed its ivied stone.
Amid the beechen wood.

Here often, when the mountain trees
A leafy murmur made,
Now still, now swaying to the breeze,
(Sounds that the musing fancy please),
The widowed mourner strayed.

And many a morn she climbed the steep,
From whence she might behold,
Where, 'neath the clouds, in shining sweep,
And mingling with the mighty deep,
The sea-broad Severn rolled.

Her little boy beside her played,
With sea-shells in his hand;
And sometimes, 'mid the bents delayed,
And sometimes running onward, said,
Oh, where is Holy Land!

My child, she cried, my prattler dear!
And kissed his light-brown hair;
Her eyelid glistened with a tear,
And none but God above could hear,
That hour, her secret prayer.

As thus she nursed her secret woes,
Oft to the wind and rain
She listened, at sad autumn's close,
Whilst many a thronging shadow rose,
Dark-glancing o'er her brain.

Now lonely to the cloudy height
Of the steep hill she strays;
Below, the raven wings his flight,
And often on the screaming kite
She sees the wild deer gaze.

The clouds were gathered on its brow,
The warring winds were high;
She heard a hollow voice, and now
She lifts to heaven a secret vow,
Whilst the king of the storm rides by.

Seated on a craggy rock,
What aged man appears!

There is no hind, no straggling flock;
Comes the strange shade my thoughts to mock,
And shake my soul with fears?

Fast drive the hurrying clouds of morn;
A pale man stands confessed;
With look majestic, though forlorn,
A mirror in his hand, and horn
Of ivory on his breast.

Daughter of grief, he gently said,
And beckoned her: come near;
Now say, what would you give to me,
If you brave Hoel's form might see,
Or the sound of his bugle hear!

Hoel, my love, where'er thou art,
All England I would give,
If, never, never more to part,
I now could hold thee to my heart,
For whom alone I live!

He placed the white horn to her ear,
And sudden a sweet voice
Stole gently, as of fairies near,
While accents soft she seemed to hear,
Daughter of grief, rejoice!

For soon to love and thee I fly,
From Salem's hallowed plain!
The mirror caught her turning eye,
As pale in death she saw him lie,
And sinking 'mid the slain.

She turned to the strange phantom-man,
But she only saw the sky,
And the clouds on the lonely mountains' van,
And the Clydden-Shoots, that rushing ran,
To meet the waves of Wye.

Thus seven long years had passed away,—
She heard no voice of mirth;
No minstrel raised his festive lay,
At the sad close of the drisly day,
Beside the blazing hearth.

She seemed in sorrow, yet serene,
No tear was on her face;

And lighting oft her pensive mien,
Upon her languid look was seen
A meek attractive grace.

In beauty's train she yet might vie,
For though in mourning weeds,
No friar, I deem, that passed her by,
Ere saw her dark, yet gentle eye,
But straight forgot his beads.

Eineon, generous and good,
Alone with friendship's aid,
Eineon, of princely Rhys's blood,
Who 'mid the bravest archers stood,
To sooth her griefs essayed.

He had himself been early tried
By stern misfortune's doom;
For she who loved him drooped and died,
And on the green hill's flowery side
He raised her grassy tomb.

What marvel, in his lonely heart,
To faith a friendship true,
If, when her griefs she did impart,
And tears of memory oft would start,
If more than pity grew.

With converse mild he oft would seek
To sooth her sense of care;
As the west wind, with breathings weak,
Wakes, on the hectic's faded cheek
A smile of faint despair.

The summer's eve was calm and still,
When once his harp he strung;
Soft as the twilight on the hill,
Affection seemed his heart to fill,
Whilst eloquent he sung:

When Fortune to all thy warm hopes was unkind,
And the morn of thy youth was o'erclouded with woe,
In me, not a stranger to grief, thou should'st find,
All that friendship and kindness and truth could bestow.

Yes, the time it has been, when my soul was oppressed,
But no longer this heart would for heaviness pine,
Could I lighten the load of an innocent breast,

And steal but a moment of sadness from thine.

He paused, then with a starting tear,
And trembling accent, cried,
O lady, hide that look severe,—
The voice of love, of friendship hear,
And be again a bride.

Mourn not thy much-loved Hoel lost,—
Lady, he is dead, is dead,—
Far distant wanders his pale ghost,—
His bones by the white surge are tossed,
And the wave rolls o'er his head.

She said, Sev'n years their course have rolled,
Since thus brave Hoel spake,
When last I heard his voice, Behold,
This ring,—it is of purest gold,—
Then, keep it for my sake.

When summers seven have robed each tree,
And decked the coombs with green,
If I come not back, then thou art free,
To wed or not, and to think of me
As I had never been.

Those seven sad summers now are o'er,
And three I yet demand;
If in that space I see no more
The friend I ever must deplore,
Then take a mourner's hand.

The time is passed:—the laugh, the lay,
The nuptial feast proclaim;
From many a rushing torrent gray,
From many a wild brook's wandering way,
The hoary minstrels came.

From Kymin's crag, with fragments strewed;
From Skirid, bleak and high;
From Penalt's shaggy solitude;
From Wyndcliff, desolate and rude,
That frowns o'er mazy Wye.

With harps the gallery glittered bright,—
The pealing rafters rung;
Far off upon the woods of night,
From the tall window's arch, the light

Of tapers clear was flung.

The harpers ceased the acclaiming lay,
When, with descending beard,
Scallop, and staff his steps to stay,
As, foot-sore, on his weary way,
A pilgrim wan appeared.

Now lend me a harp for St Mary's sake,
For my skill I fain would try,
A poor man's offering to make,
If haply still my hand may wake
Some pleasant melody.

With scoffs the minstrel crowd replied,
Dost thou a harp request!
And loud in mirth, and swelled with pride,
Some his rain-dripping hair deride,
And some his sordid vest.

Pilgrim, a harp shall soon be found,
Young Hoel instant cried;
There lies a harp upon the ground,
And none hath ever heard its sound,
Since my brave father died.

The harp is brought: upon the frame
A filmy cobweb hung;
The strings were few, yet 'twas the same;
The old man drawing near the flame,
The chords imperfect rung:

Oh! cast every care to the wind,
And dry, best beloved, the tear;
Secure that thou ever shalt find
The friend of thy bosom sincere.

She speechless gazed:—he stands confessed,—
The dark eyes of her Hoel shine;
Her heart has forgotten it e'er was oppressed,
And she murmurs aloud, as she sinks on his breast,
Oh! press my heart to thine.

He turned his look a little space,
To hide the tears of joy;
Then rushing, with a warm embrace,
Cried, as he kissed young Hoel's face,
My boy, my heart-loved boy!

Proud harpers, strike a louder lay,—
No more forlorn I bend!
Prince Eineon, with the rest, be gay,
Though fate hath torn a bride away,
Accept a long-lost friend.

This tale I heard, when at the close of day
The village harper tuned an ancient lay;
He struck his harp, beneath a ruin hoar,
And sung of love and truth, in days of yore,
And I retained the song, with counsel sage,
To teach one lesson to a wiser age!

AVENUE IN SAVERNAKE FOREST

How soothing sound the gentle airs that move
The innumerable leaves, high overhead,
When autumn first, from the long avenue,
That lifts its arching height of ancient shade,
Steals here and there a leaf!

Within the gloom,
In partial sunshine white, some trunks appear,
Studding the glens of fern; in solemn shade
Some mingle their dark branches, but yet all,
All make a sad sweet music, as they move,
Not undelightful to a stranger's heart.
They seem to say, in accents audible,
Farewell to summer, and farewell the strains
Of many a lithe and feathered chorister,
That through the depth of these incumbent woods
Made the long summer gladsome.

I have heard
To the deep-mingling sounds of organs clear,
(When slow the choral anthem rose beneath),
The glimmering minster, through its pillared aisles,
Echo;—but not more sweet the vaulted roof
Rang to those linked harmonies, than here
The high wood answers to the lightest breath
Of nature.

Oh, may such sweet music steal,
Soothing the cares of venerable age,
From public toil retired: may it awake,

As, still and slow, the sun of life declines,
Remembrances, not mournful, but most sweet;
May it, as oft beneath the sylvan shade
Their honoured owner strays, come like the sound
Of distant seraph harps, yet speaking clear!
How poor is every sound of earthly things,
When heaven's own music waits the just and pure!

DIRGE OF NELSON

Toll Nelson's knell! a soul more brave
Ne'er triumphed on the green-sea wave!
Sad o'er the hero's honoured grave,
Toll Nelson's knell!

The ball of Death unerring flew;
His cheek has lost its ardent hue;
He sinks, amid his gallant crew!
Toll Nelson's knell!

Yet lift, brave chief, thy dying eyes;
Hark! loud huzzas around thee rise;
Aloft the flag of conquest flies!
The day is won!

The day is won—peace to the brave!
But whilst the joyous streamers wave,
We'll think upon the victor's grave!
Peace to the brave!

DEATH OF CAPTAIN COOKE, OF "THE BELLEROPHON," KILLED IN THE SAME BATTLE

When anxious Spain, along her rocky shore,
From cliff to cliff returned the sea-fight's roar;
When flash succeeding flash, tremendous broke
The haze incumbent, and the clouds of smoke,
As oft the volume rolled away, thy mien,
Thine eye, serenely terrible, was seen,
My gallant friend.—Hark! the shrill bugle calls,
Is the day won! alas, he falls—he falls!
His soul from pain, from agony release!
Hear his last murmur, Let me die in peace!
Yet still, brave Cooke, thy country's grateful tear,
Shall wet the bleeding laurel on thy bier.

But who shall wake to joy, through a long life
Of sadness, thy beloved and widowed wife,
Who now, perhaps, thinks how the green seas foam,
That bear thy victor ship impatient home!
Alas! the well-known views,—the swelling plain,
Thy laurel-circled home, endeared in vain,
The brook, the church, those chestnuts darkly-green,
Yon fir-crowned summit, and the village scene,
Wardour's long sweep of woods, the nearer mill,
And high o'er all, the turrets of Font Hill:
These views, when summer comes, shall charm no more
Him o'er whose welt'ring corse the wild waves roar,
Enough: 'twas Honour's voice that awful cried,
Glory to him who for his country died!
Yet dreary is her solitude who bends
And mourns the best of husbands, fathers, friends!
Oh! when she wakes at midnight, but to shed
Fresh tears of anguish on her lonely bed,
Thinking on him who is not; then restrain
The tear, O God, and her sad heart sustain!
Giver of life, may she remember still
Thy chastening hand, and to thy sovereign will
Bow silently; not hopeless, while her eye
She raises to a bright futurity,
And meekly trusts, in heaven, Thou wilt restore
That happiness the world can give no more!

BATTLE OF CORRUNA

The tide of fate rolls on!—heart-pierced and pale,
The gallant soldier lies, nor aught avail,
The shield, the sword, the spirit of the brave,
From rapine's armed hand thy vales to save,
Land of illustrious heroes, who, of yore,
Drenched the same plains with the invader's gore,
Stood frowning, in the front of death, and hurled
Defiance to the conquerors of the world!
Oh, when we hear the agonising tale
Of those who, faint, and fugitive, and pale,
Saw hourly, harassed through their long retreat,
Some worn companion sinking at their feet,
Yet even in danger and from toil more bold,
Back on their gathering foes the tide of battle rolled;—
While tears of pity mingle with applause,
On the dread scene in silence let us pause;
Yes, pause, and ask, Is not thy awful hand

Stretched out, O God, o'er a devoted land,
Whose vales of beauty Nature spread in vain,
Where misery moaned on the uncultured plain,
Where Bigotry went by with jealous scowl,
Where Superstition muttered in his cowl;
Whilst o'er the Inquisition's dismal holds,
Its horrid banner waved in bleeding folds!
And dost thou thus, Lord of all might, fulfil
With wreck and tempests thy eternal will,
Shatter the arms in which weak kingdoms trust,
And strew their scattered ensigns in the dust?
Oh, if no human wisdom may withstand
The terrors, Lord, of thy uplifted hand;
If the dark tide no prowess can control,
Yet nearer, charged with dread commission, roll;
Still may my country's ark majestic ride,
Though sole, yet safe, on the conflicting tide;
Till hushed be the wild rocking of the blast,
And the red storm of death be overpast!

SKETCH FROM BOWDEN HILL AFTER SICKNESS

How cheering are thy prospects, airy hill,
To him who, pale and languid, on thy brow
Pauses, respiring, and bids hail again
The upland breeze, the comfortable sun,
And all the landscape's hues! Upon the point
Of the descending steep I stand.

How rich,
How mantling in the gay and gorgeous tints
Of summer! far beneath me, sweeping on,
From field to field, from vale to cultured vale,
The prospect spreads its crowded beauties wide!
Long lines of sunshine, and of shadow, streak
The farthest distance; where the passing light
Alternate falls, 'mid undistinguished trees,
White dots of gleamy domes, and peeping towers,
As from the painter's instant touch, appear.
As thus the eye ranges from hill to hill,
Here white with passing sunshine, there with trees
Innumerable shaded, clustering more,
As the long vale retires, the ample scene,
Warm with new grace and beauty, seems to live.
Lives! all is animation! beauty! hope!
Snatched from the dark and dreamless grave, so late,

Shall I pass silent, now first issuing forth,
To feel again thy fragrance, to respire
Thy breath, to hail thy look, thy living look,
O Nature!

Let me the deep joy contrast,
Which now the inmost heart like music fills,
With the sick chamber's sorrows, oft from morn,
Silent, till lingering eve, save when the sound
Of whispers steal, and bodings breathed more low,
As friends approach the pillow: so awaked
From deadly trance, the sick man lifts his eyes,
Then in despondence closes them on all,
All earth's fond wishes! Oh, how changed are now
His thoughts! he sees rich nature glowing round,
He feels her influence! languid with delight,
And whilst his eye is filled with transient fire,
He almost thinks he hears her gently say,
Live, live! O Nature, thee, in the soft winds,
Thee, in the soothing sound of summer leaves,
When the still earth lies sultry; thee, methinks,
Ev'n now I hear bid welcome to thy vales
And woods again!

And I will welcome them,
And pour, as erst, the song of heartfelt praise.
From yonder line, where fade the farthest hills
Which bound the blue lap of the swelling vale,
On whose last line, seen like a beacon, hangs
Thy tower, benevolent, accomplished Hoare,
To where I stand, how wide the interval!
Yet instantaneous, to the hurrying eye
Displayed; though peeping towers and villages
Thick scattered, 'mid the intermingling elms,
And towns remotely marked by hovering smoke,
And grass-green pastures with their herds, and seats
Of rural beauty, cottages and farms,
Unnumbered as the hedgerows, lie between!
Roaming at large to where the gray sky bends,
The eye scarce knows to rest, till back recalled
By yonder ivied cloisters in the plain,
Whose turret, peeping pale above the shade,
Smiles in the venerable grace of years.
As the few threads of age's silver hairs,
Just sprinkled o'er the forehead, lend a grace
Of saintly reverence, seemly, though compared
With blooming Mary's tresses like the morn;
So the gray weather-stained towers yet wear

A secret charm impressive, though opposed
To views in verdure flourishing, the woods,
And scenes of Attic taste, that glitter near.
O venerable pile, though now no more
The pensive passenger, at evening, hears
The slowly-chanted vesper; or the sounds
Of "Miserere," die along the vale;
Yet piety and honoured age retired,
There hold their blameless sojourn, ere the bowl
Be broken, or the silver chord be loosed.
Nor can I pass, snatched from untimely fate,
Without a secret prayer, that so my age,
When many a circling season has declined,
In charity and peace may wait its close.
Yet still be with me, O delightful friend,
Soothing companion of my vacant hours,
Oh, still be with me, Spirit of the Muse!
Not to subdue, or hold in moody spell,
The erring senses, but to animate
And warm my heart, where'er the prospect smiles,
With Nature's fairest views; not to display
Vain ostentations of a poet's art,
But silent, and associate of my joys
Or sorrows, to infuse a tenderness,
A thought, that seems to mingle, as I gaze,
With all the works of GOD. So cheer my path,
From youth to sober manhood, till the light
Of evening smile upon the fading scene.
And though no pealing clarion swell my fame,
When all my days are gone; let me not pass,
Like the forgotten clouds of yesterday,
Nor unremembered by the fatherless
Of the loved village where my bones are laid.

SUN-DIAL, IN THE CHURCHYARD OF BREMHILL

So passes silent o'er the dead thy shade,
Brief Time; and hour by hour, and day by day,
The pleasing pictures of the present fade,
And like a summer vapour steal away!

And have not they, who here forgotten lie
(Say, hoary chronicler of ages past!)
Once marked thy shadow with delighted eye,
Nor thought it fled, how certain, and how fast!

Since thou hast stood, and thus thy vigil kept,
Noting each hour, o'er mouldering stones beneath;
The pastor and his flock alike have slept,
And dust to dust proclaimed the stride of death.

Another race succeeds, and counts the hour,
Careless alike; the hour still seems to smile,
As hope, and youth, and life, were in our power;
So smiling and so perishing the while.

I heard the village bells, with gladsome sound,
When to these scenes a stranger I drew near,
Proclaim the tidings to the village round,
While memory wept upon the good man's bier.

Even so, when I am dead, shall the same bells
Ring merrily, when my brief days are gone;
While still the lapse of time thy shadow tells,
And strangers gaze upon my humble stone!

Enough, if we may wait in calm content,
The hour that bears us to the silent sod;
Blameless improve the time that heaven has lent,
And leave the issue to thy will, O God!

William Lisle Bowles – A Short Biography

William Lisle Bowles was born on 24th September 1762 at King's Sutton in Northamptonshire.

His great-grandfather, grandfather and his father, William Thomas Bowles, had all been parish priests and inevitably Bowles would join their line.

At the age of 14 he entered Winchester College, where the headmaster was Dr Joseph Warton (a minor poet, his most notable piece is The Enthusiast, 1744. In 1755, he taught at Winchester and from 1766 to 1793 was headmaster. His career as a critic was illustrious. He produced editions of poets such as Virgil as well as several English poets).

In 1789 Bowles published, a small quarto volume, Fourteen Sonnets, which was received with extraordinary praise, not only by the general public, but by such revered poets as Samuel Taylor Coleridge and Wordsworth.

The Sonnets were a return to an older and purer poetic style, and by their grace of expression, lyrical versification, tender tone of feeling and vivid appreciation of the wonder and beauty of nature, stood out in marked contrast to the elaborate works which then formed the bulk of English poetry.

Bowles said "Poetic trifles from solitary rambles whilst chewing the cud of sweet and bitter fancy, written from memory, confined to fourteen lines, this seemed best adapted to the unity of sentiment, the verse flowed in unpremeditated harmony as my ear directed but are far from being mere elegiac couplets".

The young Samuel Taylor Coleridge felt obliged to record his debt of gratitude to Bowles: "My obligations to Mr. Bowles were indeed important, and for radical good. At a very premature age, ... I had bewildered myself in metaphysicks, and in theological controversy. Nothing else pleased me. Poetry ... became insipid to me.... This preposterous pursuit was, beyond doubt, injurious both to my natural powers, and to the progress of my education.... But from this I was auspiciously withdrawn, chiefly by the genial influence of a style of poetry, so tender and yet so manly, so natural and real, and yet so dignified and harmonious, as the sonnets &c. of Mr. Bowles!"

In 1781 Bowles left as captain of Winchester school, and proceeded to Trinity College, Oxford, after winning a scholarship. Two years later he won the Chancellor's prize for Latin verse. It was now evident that the Church and poetry were to be his two callings.

After receiving his degree at Oxford, Bowles now began his career in service to the Church of England. In 1792, after serving as curate in Donhead St Andrew, Bowles was appointed vicar of Chicklade in Wiltshire.

Five years later, in 1797, he received the vicarage of Dumbleton in Gloucestershire, and in 1804 became vicar of Bremhill in Wiltshire, where he wrote the poem seen on Maud Heath's statue. In the same year his bishop, John Douglas, collated him to a prebendal stall in Salisbury Cathedral.

In 1818 Bowles was made chaplain to the Prince Regent, and in 1828 he was elected residentiary canon of Salisbury.

His years of service perhaps diminished both his stature as a poet and certainly the way he was viewed. For much of his career Bowles was seen as rather soft when set against his contemporaries but in the end his ability as a poet was enshrined, after a long and ferocious attack against him, by the principles he so eloquently wrote about and adhered too.

It is as well to remember that when critics suggest that compared to other poets his longer works were not to the standard that the competition achieved, that this era is perhaps without poetic equal. Set against Byron, Shelley, Keats, Wordsworth and other great luminaries of the era it is perhaps difficult to see his works in isolation for their own value.

The longer poems published by Bowles are distinguished by purity of imagination, cultured and graceful diction, and a great thoughtfulness of feeling. Among them were The Spirit of Discovery (1804), which alas was so mercilessly ridiculed by Byron; The Missionary (1813); The Grave of the Last Saxon (1822); and St John in Patmos (1833).

In 1806 he published an edition of Alexander Pope's works with notes and an essay, in which he laid down certain canons as to poetic imagery which, subject to some modification, were later accepted, but received at the time with strong opposition by admirers of Pope.

Bowles restated his views in 1819, in The Invariable Principles of Poetry. The controversy brought into sharp contrast the opposing views of poetry, which may be thought of as being either the natural or the artificial.

In personality and nature Bowles was said to be an amiable, absent-minded, but rather eccentric man. His poems speak warmly of a refinement of feeling, tenderness, and pensive thought, but are lacking in power and passion. But that should not diminish their value or appreciation to us.

Bowles maintained that images drawn from nature are poetically finer than those drawn from art; and that in the highest kinds of poetry the themes or passions handled should be of the general or elemental kind, and not the transient manners of any society. These positions were attacked by Byron, Thomas Campbell, William Roscoe and others, and for a time Bowles had to fight his corner on his own. Soon however, William Hazlitt and the Blackwood critics came to his assistance, and on the whole Bowles had reason to congratulate himself on having established certain principles which might serve as the basis of a true method of poetical criticism, and of having inaugurated, both by precept and by example, a new era in English poetry.

As well as his poetry Bowles was also responsible for writing a Life of Bishop Ken (in two volumes, 1830–1831), Coombe Ellen and St. Michael's Mount (1798), The Battle of the Nile (1799), and The Sorrows of Switzerland (1801).

Bowles also enjoyed considerable reputation as an antiquary and his principal work in that field was Hermes Britannicus (1828).

William Lisle Bowles died on April 7th, 1850 at the age of 87.

www.ingramcontent.com/pod-product-compliance
Lightning Source LLC
Chambersburg PA
CBHW061951070426
42450CB00007BA/1193